A Quiet Revolution

A Chronicle Of Beginnings
Of Reformation in
The Southern Baptist Convention

Ernest C. Reisinger & D. Matthew Allen

Published by:
    Founders Press
    Committed to historic Southern Baptist principles
    P.O. Box 150931 Cape Coral, FL 33915
    Phone: (941) 772-1400 Fax (941) 772-1140
    Email: editor@founders.org
    Web page: http://www.founders.org

Printed in the United States of America

ISBN   0-9654955-7-4

Distributed by:
    Christian Gospel Book Service
    521 Wildwood Parkway
    Cape Coral, FL 33904
    Phone: (941) 549-3021 Fax (941) 540-7884
    Email: DonReis@mac.com

On the cover: The Boyce Library shown on the cover is the library
for the Southern Baptist Theological Seminary in Louisville,
Kentucky. James P. Boyce, the founder of Southern Seminary, is
the "grandfather" of the Founders Movement.

This work is warmly dedicated
to all those Southern Baptist pastors
who fight the good fight in the trenches,
whose hearts burn brightly for reformation
in our churches, and who are giving their
lives for the truth of God's grace.

What is Founders Ministries?

The motive of Founders Ministries is to glorify God, honor his gospel, and strengthen his churches by providing encouragement to Southern Baptists in historical, biblical, theological, practical and ecumenical studies. As the original statement of purpose for Founders Ministries (then called the Southern Baptist Founders Conference) put it:

> The purpose is to be a balanced conference in respect to doctrine and devotion expressed in the Doctrines of Grace and their experimental application to the local church, particularly in the areas of worship and witness. This is to be accomplished through engaging a variety of speakers to present formal papers, sermons, expositions, and devotions, and through the recommendation and distribution of literature consistent with the nature of the conference.
>
> The theological foundation of the conference will be the Doctrines of Grace (election, depravity, atonement, effectual calling and perseverance) and specifically related truths. These subjects will be presented doctrinally, expositionally, homiletically and historically. Each conference will concentrate on the experimental and pastoral application of the respective doctrines.

This statement was put in black and white in Euless, Texas on November 13, 1982, and for eighteen years Founders Ministries has not deviated from it. Founders Ministries has earned some credibility by operating within the parameters of this statement as to purpose, goal and motive. There has been no hidden agenda, no formal organization, nothing to join and no denominational politics. The purpose, which is to encourage pastors and churches to return to the doctrinal foundation of our first seminary as well as most of our Southern Baptist fathers, including Basil Manly and the first several presidents of the convention, has always been right up front for all these years.

Contents

INTRODUCTION

The conservative resurgence in the Southern Baptist Convention has been one of the most remarkable changes in theological direction in recent history. After decades of suffering liberalism and neo-orthodoxy in the seminaries and denominational agencies, the people in the pews and pulpits finally said "enough" and reclaimed the denominational infrastructure for orthodoxy. As a result, the Bible is now plainly established in Baptist life as the infallible and inerrant Word of God, truth, without mixture of error, inspired in whole and in all its parts. The question for many is: Where do we go from here?

Theologically, the inerrancy group now ascendant among Southern Baptists consists of a spicy blend of pragmatists, pietists, dispensationalists, Finneyite revivalists, charismatics, Arminians, Calvinists, and countless variants and combinations of each of these categories. So far at least, these divergent groups have managed to live relatively peaceably together because they share an overriding commitment to the truthfulness and authority of Scripture.

But what now? The authors of this book suggest that the crying need for Southern Baptists going forward is to apply Biblical precepts to our lives and practice. It is not enough to simply claim to be a "Bible man." Too often, this assertion masks a hostility to theology and the systematic interpretation of Scripture. We must be ruthless in the application of all the precepts of Scripture to every aspect of our lives.

At one time in our history, this point was not open to debate. At the turn of the twentieth century, Richard M. Dudley wrote in *Baptist Why and Why Not*:

> The fundamental principle of the Baptists is their belief in the supreme authority and absolute sufficiency of the Holy Scriptures; and their separate existence is the practical and logical result of their attempt to apply this principle in all matters of religion...God's Word is the supreme and infallible rule for our guidance. We must not go contrary to it in any article of belief or in any duty enjoined. It is no partial revelation. By it the man of God is thoroughly furnished unto all good works. This is the fundamental position of the Baptists, and every peculiarity which characterizes them is the practical outcome of this principle.[1]

7

Indeed, Baptists traditionally have been in the forefront of defending, not only the authority of the Bible, but also its sufficiency. This certainly was the view of the English Particular Baptists. Articles VII and VIII of the Baptist Confession of 1644 state:

> The Rule of this Knowledge, Faith and Obedience, concerning the worship and service of God, and all other Christian duties, is not man's inventions, opinions, devices, laws, constitutions, or traditions unwritten whatsoever, but only the word of God contained in the Canonical Scriptures.
>
> In this written Word of God hath plainly revealed whatsoever he hath thought needful for us to know, believe, and acknowledge, touching the Nature and Office of Christ, in whom all the promises are Yea and Amen to the praise of God.[2]

The Second London Confession of 1689 similarly states that "the Holy Scripture is the only sufficient...rule of all saving Knowledge, Faith and Obedience" and "those former ways of God's revealing his will unto his people [dreams, visions, etc.] being now ceased."[3] It emphatically declares that the "whole Council of God concerning all things necessary for his own Glory, Man's Salvation, Faith and Life is either expressly set down or necessarily contained in the Holy Scripture; unto which nothing at any time is to be added, whether by new Revelation of the Spirit, or traditions of men."[4] John Gill repeated this precept in his confession, which states that Scripture is "the only rule of faith and practice."[5] Scripture contains "the whole of God's will and pleasure toward us."[6]

American Baptists also vigorously upheld the notion of the sufficiency of Scripture. The first American Baptist, Roger Williams, said that the Bible is the "square rule" that determines "all knowledge of God and of ourselves."[7] Nineteenth century Southern Baptist theologian John Broadus wrote: "What authority has the Bible for us? The Bible is our only and all-sufficient rule of faith and practice..."[8]

An introductory statement to the 1925 Southern Baptist Faith and Message declared: "That the sole authority for faith and practice among Baptists is the Scriptures of the Old and New Testaments."[9] We are gratified that the 2000 Baptist Faith and Message signals a return to the historic Baptist defense of the sufficiency of Scripture, replacing the sentence, "The criterion by which the Bible is to be interpreted is Jesus Christ," with the sentence, "All Scripture is a testimony to Christ, who is Himself the focus of divine revelation."

These affirmations of the sufficiency of Scripture, of course, flow directly from 2 Peter 1:3: "His divine power has given us everything we need for life and godliness through our knowledge of him who called us by his own glory and goodness."

How ironic it is that, despite the courageous stand of many in favor of the plenary, verbal inspiration and inerrancy of Scripture, our churches too often pay no more than lip service to the sufficiency of Scripture by essentially ignoring what the inspired and authoritative Bible says about life, godliness, faith and practice! One English Baptist put it something like this: "You American Baptists take the Bible literally, but you don't take it seriously." What an indictment this is!

Examples of Biblical neglect abound.

Scripture clearly requires us to fulfill the Great Commission by going into all the world to make disciples (Mt. 28:18-20). Yet how many of our churches give more than lip service to evangelism to unreached people groups or to the impoverished in our own inner cities? Is our "world" so narrow that it encompasses only people "like us"?

Scripture clearly demands that local congregations engage in biblical formative and restorative church discipline of their members (Mt. 18:15-20). Yet how many Southern Baptist churches actually practice church discipline in the face of possible lawsuits by disgruntled members who have gone astray?

Scripture plainly commands ministers of the gospel to preach the Word in season and out of season—no matter how unpopular God's truth may be (2 Tim. 4:2). Yet how many Southern Baptist sermons contain precious little in the way of Biblical proclamation, but are chock full of shallow manipulation, therapeutical advice or calls for political activism? How many of our pastors are resigned to topical preaching because that is all the congregation can stand, rather than preaching exegetically, verse by verse, through a book on a regular basis?

Scripture plainly implies that prophecies and tongues and other "sign gifts" ceased at the close of the New Testament canon (Heb. 1:1-2; cf. 2 Cor. 12:12). Yet how many of our Southern Baptist churches are falling prey to dangerous charismatic influences that are unbiblical, not to mention foreign to the Baptist heritage?

These are only a few examples of how far Southern Baptists have come since 1900 when Dudley penned the words quoted above with respect to the sufficiency of Scripture. In much of our denomination, our churches have lost their biblical priority in favor of programs, marketing techniques and emotionalism. Perhaps, then, the battle for the Bible is not over. Perhaps we still have a long way to go. Could it be that we win the battle of Scripture's inerrancy only to lose the war of Scripture's sufficiency?

Yet, at the same time that many are losing their bearing amid the thickets of pragmatism, programs, and Pentecostalism, many others are finding their way back to the old paths upon which our denomination was founded. A quiet revolution is currently ongoing in Southern Baptist life.

Since the early 1970s, our denomination has seen an undeniable resurgence of interest in the theological system known as Calvinism and its attendant principles that we call the "doctrines of grace." Calvinism is a much-maligned system by those who are ignorant of its teachings. In reality, Calvinism is nothing more than biblical Christianity. It lies in a profound apprehension that God is imminently majestic, holy, beautiful, and glorious, and that God's creation is profoundly sinful and needful of redemption. Hence, it promotes an attitude of dependence on God through all the activities of life. It teaches that salvation comes only when the sinful person rests in humble, self-emptying trust in the most wonderful, amazing grace of God. These are the fundamental principles of Calvinism.[10]

The doctrines of grace, commonly called the "Five Points of Calvinism," flow from these basic tenets. These doctrines center on the fact that "salvation is of the Lord" (Jonah 2:9). They consist of the biblical teachings that:

1. Because of the fall, man is unable of himself to believe the gospel (Rom. 3:10-18). The sinner is dead, blind and deaf to the things of God (2 Cor. 4:3-4; Eph. 2:1-2). His heart is deceitful and desperately wicked (Gen. 6:5; Jer. 17:9). As the first writing Southern Baptist John Dagg said, "Depravity exists at the very fountain from which all human action flows. The depravity of man is total."[11] Calvinists call this "total depravity."

2. As a consequence of man's depravity, it is only by the Holy Spirit's special inward call that sinners can come to salvation (John 6:37, 44; 10:16; Rom. 8:29-30). The founder of the first Southern Baptist seminary, James P. Boyce, put it like this: The external call of the Gospel "meets with no success because of the willful sinfulness of man, although, in itself, it has all the elements which should secure its acceptance." But God, knowing this is true even of those he has chosen to save, "gives to these such

10

influences of the Spirit as will lead to their acceptance of the call."[12] Calvinists call this "effectual calling" or "efficacious grace." The person does nothing to initiate the saving process (John 15:16). Indeed, faith itself is a gift of God (Eph. 2:8-9).

3. Moreover, God's choice of individuals unto salvation occurred before the foundation of the world and rested solely in his sovereign will (Eph. 1:4-5, 11; Rom. 8:29-30; 9:6-26; 2 Thess. 2:13; Acts 13:48). Calvinists call this "unconditional election." As Boyce carefully put it: "God...of his own purpose (in accordance with his will, and not from any obligation to man, nor because of any will of man), has from Eternity...determined to save...a definite number of mankind...as individuals...not for or because of any merit or work of theirs, nor of any value to him of them (not for their good works, nor their holiness, nor excellence, nor their faith, nor their spiritual sanctification...nor their value to him...); but of his own good pleasure (simply because he was pleased so to choose)."[13]

4. In addition, Christ's redeeming work was designed to save the elect, and it actually secured salvation for them. Christ came not to advise or urge or induce or assist the elect to save themselves. No! He came to actually save the ones he chose (John 10:15; Rom. 3:25; 5:10). Thus, in Boyce's words, although the atonement of Christ "is abundantly sufficient to secure the salvation of all who will put their faith in him," Christ died "in an especial sense for the Elect; because he procured for them not a possible, but an actual salvation."[14] Calvinists call this "particular redemption."

5. Finally, all who are chosen by God, redeemed by Christ, and given faith by the Holy Spirit are eternally saved (Rom. 8:38-39; John 6:39; John 10:28-29; Eph. 1:13-14). The truly redeemed cannot fall from grace. In Dagg's words, "whatever struggles it may cost, and whatever temporary departures from the straight line of duty may mark their course, they are graciously preserved from total and final apostasy." Indeed, grace in the heart is "incorruptible and abiding."[15] This is called the "preservation of the saints" and its flip side, the "perseverance of the saints."

These doctrines are foundational to a God-centered theology. They are the heart of historical, orthodox Christianity. Salvation is sovereignly and graciously given by God to sinners, not on the basis of any merit of their own, but simply on the basis of God's own purpose and pleasure. They are not an end unto themselves. They are the God-ordained means by which God glorifies and magnifies himself in the salvation of those he has chosen. We glorify him as well as we recognize and acknowledge that it is God who chose us to salvation; it is God who has redeemed us from wrath, and to him we owe our entire salvation and indeed our lives. To him be the glory forever and ever!

In these days God has raised up many Southern Baptists who have become convinced of these essential truths. Many Southern Baptists are also discovering (some to delight, others to shock) that our Baptist forefathers come from hearty Calvinistic stock. Our forebears held these doctrines of grace to be extremely precious. They zealously promulgated them. They earnestly defended them. The current rediscovery of these men and their doctrines is to our great benefit.

As more and more pastors and lay leaders in the Southern Baptist denomination are laying hold of the doctrines of grace, a fire of reformation is spreading throughout our Southern Baptist ranks, a burning zeal for God's great glory, a heart cry for a return to our biblical, doctrinal roots, and a substantial interest in what one of our founders, John Broadus, called, "that exalted system of Pauline Theology, which is technically called Calvinism."

It has been a tremendous joy for the authors of this book to come to love and embrace these truths (one of us almost fifty years ago; the other less than ten years ago). We rejoice that the Southern Baptist Convention began its existence as a Calvinistic, reformed denomination. Even more so, we yearn to see the day when our vision for reformation is shared by our contemporaries and the generations to follow.

Make no mistake about it. Southern Baptists are at a crossroads. We have a choice to make. The choice is between the deep-rooted, God-centered theology of evangelical Calvinism and the man-centered, unstable theology of the other perspectives present in the convention. As for us, we adhere to the doctrines of grace because we seek nothing more than to glorify God and enjoy him forever through true doctrine and true devotion and true worship and true witness. The way we see it, to be a Calvinist is to hold to a God-magnifying faith, proclaiming that salvation is granted by grace, received by faith, grounded in Christ and reflective of the glory of God. To be a Calvinist is to be comforted by these truths, trusting that the God of the Bible, who is infinitely holy and righteous and loving, will not only save us but also keep us until the day of the coming of our Lord Jesus Christ. Calvinism is a biblical faith which lives and breathes Scripture as God's infallible, inspired, inerrant Word, living and active, powerful, and sufficient for all of life. It is a stable faith, firmly entrenched within the historic orthodox tradition, flowing from Jesus and Paul through Augustine, Luther, Calvin, Owen, Bunyan, Edwards and Whitefield. It is a conserving faith, heartily resistant to the errors that plague other evangelical viewpoints.

Our Baptist Calvinist heritage is expressed most completely in the confessions of the early English Particular Baptists: the London Confession of 1644 and the Second London Confession of 1689. We embrace those confessions. We stand with that immortal dreamer, John Bunyan, whose writings are saturated with God-honoring, Calvinistic theology. We also join Baptist missionaries William Carey, Adoniram Judson, Luther Rice and Lottie Moon, and Southern Baptist founders Basil Manly, Sr., W.B. Johnson, R.B.C. Howell, and P.H. Mell, and the "gentlemen theologians," James P. Boyce, John A. Broadus and John L. Dagg. How we rejoice to know that our beloved Baptists fall within this historical stream of biblical Christianity! It's as simple as this: If those principles were true for the founders in their day, they must be true for us today. God has not changed; the Bible has not changed.

In sum, we agree with nineteenth century Anglican Bishop J.C. Ryle, when he declared that he would stand by what he called simple, unadulterated, old-fashioned evangelical theology.[16] Like him, we yearn to walk along the "old paths" in which the apostolic Christians, the reformers, and the historic Baptists have walked. From these paths we see no reason to depart. True, they are often sneered at and ridiculed as old-fashioned, out-of-touch, worn out and useless, in the twenty-first as in the nineteenth century. Be it so. None of these things move us. The way of the modern religionist is broad, inclusive, tolerant and devoid of any truth-claim at all. But we firmly maintain that the way of the school to which we belong is the more excellent way. The longer we live the more we are convinced that the world needs no new gospel, as many conservatives and liberals alike tend to think. We are thoroughly persuaded that the world needs nothing but a bold, full, unflinching return to the "old paths." The same doctrines preached by Bunyan, Carey, Fuller, Judson, Rice, Moon, Dagg, Boyce, and Broadus—these are the doctrines which, we find, wear well; and in the faith of the Bible that teaches them, we hope to live and die. In this view, we are gratified to know that we are not alone.

This book is designed to assist pastors and other church leaders who share our vision for a return to the "old paths" and who are serious about reformation in Southern Baptist life. Our goal is to arm those individuals involved in the trenches of reforming local churches with the information needed to accomplish their purpose. We seek to answer the following questions.

Why do we need a reformation? Where have we come from? This is the subject of Chapter 1. It describes the *necessity of reformation.* How did we in the Southern Baptist Convention get to where we are today, given our glorious Reformed heritage?

Where are we going in this process of reformation? That is the topic of Chapter 2. It describes the *beginnings of reformation in Southern Baptist life* through the work of Founders Ministries. How did the Founders Movement start? What problems has it faced? We emphasize that this chapter describes only the beginnings of reformation because, as of this writing, we are in the middle of this powerful move of God in Southern Baptist life. Who can tell in which direction or how far it will go? We are excited about what God has done so far, and we pray he will continue this movement of the Holy Spirit.

What challenges will I face in local church reformation and how do I avoid shipwreck? This is the subject of Chapter 3. It discusses the means of reformation. How does God go about reforming a local church? What kind of man does he use? Where does true reformation begin? What are the costs? These are practical questions that deserve much discussion. We hope this material provides a place for that discussion to start. Some of the material in this chapter has been previously published by Ernie Reisinger. However, that material has been reworked and revised for this publication. In addition, some of the material in Chapters 2 and 3 will be published in another form in a forthcoming biography of Ernie Reisinger to be published by the Banner of Truth Trust. We offer this book now, however, in the present format, in the hope that it will meet the need of Southern Baptist reformers for both historical perspective and practical advice.

We have also included a discussion in Chapter 4 on the use of creeds, confessions and catechisms in our churches to address the question: *What tools will I have to use as I seek reformation in my church?* Sadly, these instruments of learning have been sorely neglected in the modern church, to our substantial detriment. The rediscovery of these tools of reformation and doctrinal training is much needed.

To sum up, we long for the day when the God-centered doctrines of grace, proclaimed by a great cloud of witnesses—John Bunyan, George Whitefield, Jonathan Edwards, Charles Spurgeon, James Boyce, Basil Manly, John Broadus, B. H. Carroll, William Carey, Adoniram Judson and Luther Rice—thunder through America again. An early English Baptist, Benjamin Keach, said long ago, "Reformation is a glorious work, and it is what we all long and breathe after." Keach was right. Reformation is a glorious work. And it is a much-needed work. It is the next

Southern Baptist challenge. May God be pleased to continue this quiet revolution in the Southern Baptist Convention and beyond! May he continue opening the eyes of others, even as he opened our own eyes! As the Psalmist prayed, "Open my eyes that I may see wonderful things in your law" (Ps. 119:18).

Ernest C. Reisinger
D. Matthew Allen

CHAPTER ONE

The Need for Reformation
In The Southern Baptist Convention

How We Lost Our Way Along the Path

The chief ground
of gladness and joy is,
When God restores to us
pure and sound doctrine;
For no scarcity of wheat
ought to terrify and alarm us
As a scarcity of the word.

John Calvin

Our Present Condition

On July 7-10, 1941, Martyn Lloyd-Jones, the famed physician-turned-minister of Westminster Chapel, spoke at a private conference of distinguished English evangelicals at Kingham Hill School near Oxford, England. The attendees had gathered to discuss the downward slide of theology in British evangelicalism. Lloyd-Jones was assigned to deliver one of the main addresses. "The Doctor," as he was affectionately called, believed that the evangelicalism of his day was in serious difficulty. He was deeply concerned that the dearth of theology in the pulpits and colleges would severely weaken evangelicalism in the years to come. Yet he also believed the leaders of the evangelical movement were unaware of the grave danger. It, therefore, fell upon him to provide a meaningful diagnosis. In his address, with surgical precision, Lloyd-Jones explicated what he considered to be the most pressing theological problems in the church of his day: (1) The liberal church was anemic because it substituted philosophy for theology. (2) The evangelical church was weak because it ignored biblical scholarship. (3) Indeed, up to 90 percent of evangelicals were not concerned about doctrine. Instead, they were wrapped up in subjectivity and experience as lodestars for their faith. (4) Thus, biblical theology and accurate exegesis were absent from all liberal and most evangelical preaching. (5) Most evangelicals lacked any system of theology at all, and even resisted the use of logic in thinking of spiritual things. After laying out these points, Lloyd-Jones then traced these weaknesses back to their historical sources.[17] He believed that if the Christian leaders received an accurate diagnosis of the problem, they could then look for an applicable cure.

The parallels with American Christianity today are striking. As we enter the twenty-first century, it is not difficult to observe that evangelicalism in our country is also in serious trouble. Numerous observers have warned us over the last ten years that American evangelicals have all but forsaken their biblical and theological heritage.[18]

David Wells, in particular, has demonstrated with devastating detail that, in today's typical evangelical church, the unchanging foundation of the Word of God has been replaced by the ever-changing assumptions of modernity. Thus, the modern church values pragmatics over the eternal verities of the Word of God. Our preachers peddle pop psychology, rather than the healing balm of Christ's redemption. Our sermons are relevant, topical, humorous, poignant, dramatic—anything but biblical. Theology itself has been dismissed as irrelevant, dusty and unimportant.

Unfortunately, in all too many pulpits, these are not generalizations. They are true.

This retreat from Biblical preaching in evangelicalism is especially ironic, given that the hallmark phrase of America's best-known evangelical, Billy Graham, is "The Bible says..." Indeed, in the 1950s, Carl F. H. Henry, the first editor of *Christianity Today*, could assert with confidence and vigor: "'The Bible says' is not a mere Graham platitude nor a fundamentalist cliché: it is the note of authority in Protestant preaching, lost by the meandering modernism of the past generation, held fast by the evangelical movement."[19] At that time, evangelicalism could at least mount an argument for the right to claim the mantle of the sixteenth century reformation over and against the enlightenment and all that it embodies. Now, evangelicalism itself is lost in a morass of meandering modernism.

Examples that shock the conscience are not hard to find. The seeker-sensitive movement, by its very nature, is a bow to modernistic assumptions. Thus, many churches are now offering Friday night or Saturday night services to replace or supplement the Sunday morning worship time. Why? So church members can now get church out of the way early, then have the rest of the weekend to use as they wish. One Saturday churchgoer explained, "If you go to Sunday school at 9:00 A.M., then to the 11 A.M. service and leave about 1 P.M., your day is pretty well shot."[20] Other seeker-sensitive churches have decided to forego offering communion as part of their worship services. Instead, they provide worshipers the opportunity to partake of the elements as they walk out the door after the conclusion of the service. Why? So that those who have not committed to Christianity will not feel excluded by the process. Others, using the same logic, go the opposite direction and invite Christians and non-Christians alike to partake of the Lord's Table, hoping that the drinking of the cup and eating of the wafer will assist in making unbelievers feel comfortable with this basic Christian ritual.

Many seeker services have even given up on preaching, offering instead dramatic skits, modern music, multimedia and other means of communication to entertain the audience. Even if preaching is offered, it is typically packaged in short, fifteen to twenty minute "talks" or "discussions" attempting to show that Christianity is a comfortable religion and Christians are "OK" people—normal, just like every one else in the world.

In his book *Ashamed of the Gospel*, John MacArthur cites the following examples from newspaper clippings about the preaching of seeker-sensitive churches:

There is no fire and brimstone here. No Bible-thumping. Just practical, witty messages.

Services at [name omitted] have an informal feeling. You won't hear people threatened with hell or referred to as sinners. The goal is to make them feel welcome, not drive them away.

As with all clergymen, [name omitted]'s answer is God—but he slips Him in at the end, and even then doesn't get heavy. No ranting, no raving. No fire, no brimstone. He doesn't even use the H-word. Call it Light Gospel. It has the same salvation as the Old Time Religion, but with a third less guilt.

The sermons are relevant, upbeat, and best of all, short. You won't hear a lot of preaching about sin and damnation and hell fire. Preaching here doesn't sound like preaching. It is sophisticated, urbane, and friendly talk. It breaks all the stereotypes.

[Name omitted] is preaching a very upbeat message....It's a salvationist message, but the idea is not so much being saved from the fires of hell. Rather, it's being saved from meaninglessness and aimlessness in this life. It's more of a soft-sell.

The idea, [name omitted] says, is to get people through the front doors, then disprove the stereotype of the sweating, loosened necktied, Bible-thumping preacher who yells and screams about burning in hell for eternity.[21]

Each of us can probably add our own examples to MacArthur's list.

Of course, it is not just the seeker-sensitive crowd that has abandoned expositional preaching. The charismatic churches have replaced the eternal prescription of "thus sayeth the Lord" with emotionalism, sensationalism, and a God-as-a-bellhop mentality. The pragmatic churches have replaced sound doctrinal teaching with a plethora of five and seven step programs heavy-laden with the best contemporary notions psychology and marketing have to offer, sprinkled of course with a few out-of-context Bible verses, on virtually every subject—from salvation to dieting, from parenting to treatment of depression.

Thus, despite the variety of approaches offered by these perspectives, the bottom line is that Scripture is decentralized, hard truths are ignored, sin is soft peddled, and grace is perverted. It is not an exaggeration to say that modern evangelicalism has traded its Scriptural birthright for a mess of modern, cultural pottage. Our preaching, our evangelism, our music and our worship have become self-centered rather than God-centered. As a consequence, evangelicalism has lost its passion for God.

These same trends are evident in our own Southern Baptist Convention. Paige Patterson made this point early in 2000 at a conference designed to articulate the fundamentals of the faith for the twenty-first century. In the keynote address he cited the shallowness of the evangelical pulpit and the shallowness of praise and worship as causes for concern. He warned, "If we don't do better, we will raise a generation of theological illiterates." He proclaimed that the church today needs preachers who will explicate the word of God verse by verse, explaining the truth of the Bible.[22] Patterson is absolutely right, at least in his diagnosis.

The problems are well known. First, many of our churches have a weak theology. Consider, for example, the doctrine of salvation. In many Southern Baptist churches, regeneration (or being born again) has simply lost its meaning. No longer does it refer to a divine act of the Holy Spirit in giving a sinner a new heart and a new life, and bringing that person from spiritual death to spiritual life. Instead, being born again is simply a synonym for what happens when a person "makes a decision to accept Jesus Christ into his heart as personal Savior." Or worse, it means to "come forward" or "walk down an aisle."

This was driven home to one of us (Allen) forcefully recently when a friend casually mentioned that his brother-in-law wanted to get saved, but he had to wait until Sunday when he could go to the local Baptist church and "walk forward" to the front to receive Christ. It apparently did not occur to him that he could believe and repent and be converted in his own home. Still further, the common twentieth century Baptist view of eternal security is fundamentally flawed. We dip 'em and drop 'em, and take comfort in the fact that they are saved even though they never darken the door of a church again. After all, "once saved, always saved." In this way, we ignore—to the eternal loss of many—that the flip side of God's preservation of the saints is the biblical teaching of the saint's perseverance in Christ. We have forgotten the historic Baptist belief that those who do not persevere are not carnal Christians; they are not Christians at all!

Predictably, this weak theology leads to weak evangelism. Much of what is called evangelism in our Baptist churches is shallow, manipulative and decision-focused. The principal tools of the trade are altar calls (in which the pump is primed by well-placed counselors who set the example in walking to the front of the church) and the "sinner's prayer," in which the person "invites Christ into his life." Then, we give immediate assurance to the person who prays the "sinner's prayer" that he or she is eternally secure in salvation. Never mind the life and practice tests of 1 John. (Cf. 1 John 5:13; "I write these things to you who believe in the name of the Son of God so that you may know that you have eternal life.").

Of course, the inherent result of a weak soteriology and weak evangelism is a weak membership. We base membership on a "profession of faith," rather than evidence of a changed life. Our churches baptize preschoolers and accept professions of faith from couples living in open sin. By inviting so-called carnal Christians into our fellowships, we populate our rolls with unregenerate church members.

The result of a weak membership is a demand for weak worship. Our congregations have not learned to go beyond the pabulum of shallow praise choruses so prevalent in our worship services today. The self-centered nature of these choruses is manifest. The one doing the praising is more central than the one praised in such choruses as "I Bless You," "I Just Want to Praise You," "I Only Want to Love You" and so on.[23] This is not God-exalting worship! It is man exalting! Woe to those who are more impressed with our "love for God" than God's love for us!

One newspaper advertisement for a church in Tampa, Florida boasts of its "casual worship." What an oxymoron this is! How can worship—acknowledging the "worth-ship" of Jesus Christ, the Holy One, God of very God, light of very light—be casual? This type of worship approach is defended as an attempt to be all things to all people. What it really represents is an attempt to co-opt the world's values. For churches that have lost their biblical moorings, adapting worship practices to the world is not an irrational response to a worldly church membership. The problem, of course, is that it is an acutely unbiblical response.

Given these appalling facts, is it any wonder that the greatest segment of converts to the Mormon church comes from Southern Baptist congregations? And, is it any wonder that most of our Southern Baptist churches have a stagnant or declining membership? The Wall Street Journal reported in 1990 that, of the 14.9 million members of Southern Baptist churches (according to an official count), over 4.4 million are "non-resident members." This

23

means they are members with whom the church has lost touch. Another 3 million hadn't attended church or donated to a church in the past year. That left about 7.4 million "active" members. However, according to Sunday School consultant Glenn Smith, even this is misleading, because included in this "active" figure are those members who only attended once a year at Easter or Christmas.[24] The only conclusion to be drawn is that our Southern Baptist Convention is a denomination of unregenerate church members!

This, then, is the diagnosis: contemporary evangelical churches as a whole, and a large number of Southern Baptist churches as a subset (dare I say the majority?), are devoid of biblical and theological thinking, have abandoned a high view of the sufficiency of Scripture, and have traded in biblical values for modern notions of modernity. In our judgment, evangelicalism is collapsing of its own weight.

How We Got To Where We Are Today

What, then, is the prescription? Before we look at the cure for our present condition, we must first understand how we got here. One of the defining marks of modern man is a slender sense of history. We will never understand where we are today without also understanding how we got here. This is because the present condition has its roots in the past. It is a product of the errors of the past.

Where did we go wrong? How did we go wrong?

One answer that is often given is that our ministers no longer preach expositionally. There is too much topical preaching and too much psychological preaching. This was the answer Paige Patterson offered at the 2000 "Fundamentals" conference.

Another answer is that we have lost sight of the holiness of God. Contrary to modern notions, love is not the only attribute of God that bears on the question of who will be saved and on what basis. Holiness matters because God's eyes are too pure to look upon sin (Hab. 1:13). Holiness matters because, without holiness, no one will see God (Heb. 12:14).

Still another answer is that we have grown too self-centered. We think too highly of ourselves. Thus, modern man believes he is deserving of God's mercy and that God must simply excuse his sin.

Another answer is that twenty-first century Christians have lost the capacity to believe in ultimate truth. Contemporary notions of truth as relative have crept into the church. Thus, we have couples living together outside of marriage wanting to join the church and getting upset when the church won't admit them into membership without repentance and a change of lifestyle.

Yet another answer, and a related one, is that American Christians have lost an understanding of the law as a necessary precursor to salvation. The Puritans believed in law preaching because they understood that the gospel is meaningful only to sinners who recognize their sinfulness. They recognized that the Holy Spirit ordinarily uses a confrontation with the demands of the law to bring sinners to know their helplessness before God and their need for salvation (cf. Mt. 19:16-22).[25]

Still another answer is that we have lost our emphasis on doctrine and theology, choosing instead to focus on the "practical" application of Scripture—without the doctrinal content from which the practical application should flow. As David Wells has put it, "the anti-theological mood that now grips the evangelical world" is "severing the link to historical, Protestant orthodoxy."[26]

All of these answers are true. And yet, none is complete. The heart of the matter is that evangelicals lost their way when they abandoned the God-centered doctrinal foundation of Calvinistic theology and replaced it with a theological stew of man-centered belief systems. In other words, the evangelical church lost her stability when she deserted her theological roots in the doctrines of grace. As Charles Spurgeon observed during the English Baptist Downgrade Controversy in the late nineteenth century, Calvinism is an inherently stabilizing force in orthodox Christianity.

As discussed earlier, evangelical Calvinism is biblical Christianity. Therefore, it takes the Word of God seriously, as the very words of God. Its hallmarks include a Godward theology, an emphasis on the holiness of God, the preaching of the law as a means of pointing to grace, an emphasis on repentance as an element of conversion, and the use of expository preaching.

Yet all would agree that only a minority of Baptist churches consider themselves "Calvinistic" in orientation. We have wandered far from these "old paths" that our founders used to walk.

When did the great shift from our doctrinal foundation take place? In English Baptist life it has been persuasively argued that the "downgrade" (as Charles Spurgeon called it) began in the early nineteenth century, when the Baptist Union got rid of its Calvinistic statement of faith in favor of a watered-down, broadly evangelistic confession to which Arminian Baptists could happily subscribe.[27] In American evangelicalism at-large, the downgrade probably occurred in the middle years of the nineteenth century. Mark Noll has made the case that modernism entered American Christianity through the universities during this time frame.[28]

Several factors led to this advance. The first was a revolution in American higher education in the latter part of the nineteenth century. The 1870s saw an amazing influx of funding for older universities such as Yale, Princeton, Harvard and Columbia, and newer universities such as Johns Hopkins, Stanford and Chicago. Much of this funding came from wealthy entrepreneurs such as Ezra Cornell, Cornelius Vanderbilt and John D. Rockefeller. As more money came into the universities, so did more students. Nearly unnoticed amid this great influx of dollars and students was the steady weakening of traditional Christian influence. In 1886 at Harvard, compulsory chapel attendance was abolished. Businessmen replaced clergymen on boards of trustees and professional educators replaced ministers as university presidents. Another part of the academic revolution was the growing appeal of the German model of academic life, which emphasized the priority of specialized, advanced scholarship over the traditional emphasis in the universities of character formation.

The second factor was the rise of Darwinism. Charles Darwin published his *Origin of the Species* in 1859. By postulating that the universe came into existence by random chance, Darwin's theory of evolution questioned the legitimacy of pointing to the design of the universe as a proof of God's existence. In addition, Darwin's successors, Herbert Spencer and Thomas Huxley, suggested that evolutionary theories could provide a framework for a whole philosophy of life. In their view, humanity was inexorably advancing from the simple to the more complex, from the primitive to a sophisticated state of existence. In this view, while Christianity may have helped primitives to cope, moderns could do fine without it. In fact, Andrew D. White, the first president of Cornell University, argued in a book entitled *A History of the Warfare of Science with Theology in Christendom* (1895) that organized religion actually stymied the advance of science and therefore the progress of humanity! Many Christians of the late nineteenth century sought to accommodate Christian faith to a belief in some form of evolution. Sadly, among them were Princeton theologian B.B. Warfield and northern Baptist A.H. Strong.

As a result of all this, American seminaries were open to new approaches to interpreting Scripture, particularly the new "higher critical" theories that had come over from Germany. These theories transformed the Bible from the God-revealed source of authority for faith, practice and life into "a problem demanding increasing attention and generally increasing controversy."[29]

Fortunately (and providentially) Southern Baptists were largely immune to inroads from theological liberalism. This was due to several reasons.

26

First, Southern Baptists were still largely located in the reconstructed South. As a result, they were more isolated than their northern brethren and, therefore, more unified.

Second, unlike their English Baptist counterparts, Southern Baptists had not watered down their confessions of faith, many still holding strongly to the Philadelphia Confession, a slight modification of the Second London Confession of 1689, or the New Hampshire Declaration of Faith, an only somewhat less Calvinistic confession of faith.

Third, Southern Baptists generally had not watered down their doctrinal Calvinism. They still walked along the old paths that acted as an inherent check on theological meanderings. As John Broadus declared in 1891:

> The people who sneer at what is called Calvinism might as well sneer at Mont Blanc. We are not in the least bound to defend all of Calvin's opinions or actions, but I do not see how anyone who really understands the Greek of the Apostle Paul or the Latin of Calvin and Turretin can fail to see that these latter did not interpret and formulate substantially what the former teaches.[30]

Fourth, James P. Boyce and the other founders of Southern Seminary (at that time, the only Southern Baptist seminary) had the foresight to establish the Abstract of Principles as its statement of faith and require faculty members to agree to its tenets before being allowed to teach at the seminary. This ensured that Southern Baptist pastors, in their training, learned nothing but orthodox doctrine.[31]

Thus, in our own Southern Baptist Convention, the shift occurred later, in the early years of the twentieth century. In 1899, Southern Seminary professor E. C. Dargan could still write, in a small book published by the Sunday School Board and designed to teach basic doctrine to Baptist young people, that election was God choosing those who will be saved, that God made his choice before the foundation of the world, and that God's choice in election is not on the basis of foreseen faith or repentance, but God's sovereign, free, untrammeled, gracious acting on his own initiative.[32] Similarly, in 1900, J.M. Frost, first president of the Sunday School Board, could still write that "Baptists are one in contending for the faith; one in their history and in the heritage of their fathers; one in their purpose to preach the gospel of the grace of God among all nations...."[33] This unity, however, would not last long into the new century.

It has been said that a cataclysmic shift occurred in the seventeenth century in the area of philosophical thought, when Rene Descartes taught that the starting point of all knowledge was not God but man. Through his famous *cognito ergo sum* ("I think, therefore I am"), the individual consciousness was set up as the final criterion of truth. Centuries later, a no less monumental shift occurred in the realm of theological thought in the Baptist world. Through the dynamic leadership of Edgar Young Mullins, the starting point of theological reflection was shifted from God to the self. This departure from the shared Calvinist heritage of the past has had disastrous consequences that are still with us today.

Winston Churchill once said of the Soviet Union that it was riddle wrapped in an enigma inside a mystery. The same could be said for E. Y. Mullins. Mullins virtually single-handedly kept the SBC a calm place to be as the storm of the modernist controversy raged in other denominations. Yet, at the same time, his own theology of experience moved the denomination away from the Calvinism of the past and contributed to the storm's inevitable coming to the SBC after Mullins' lifetime of service had been completed.

Mullins was born January 5, 1860, in Franklin County, Mississippi. His father Seth Mullins was a Baptist preacher and schoolteacher. When reconstruction hit Mississippi after the Civil War, Seth Mullins moved his family to Corsicana, Texas.

Mullins early demonstrated a love for learning and reading, inspired by his father's example. He entered the first cadet class at Texas A&M at age 16. After graduation, he worked as a telegraph operator to save money for a legal education. He showed no interest in following in his father's footsteps. In fact, Mullins was not converted until 1880, when he attended worship services in Dallas. He was shortly thereafter baptized by his father at the Corsicana church. A few months later Mullins felt a "definite call to the ministry," and within the year he had departed for Southern Baptist Theological Seminary. There, Mullins studied under James Boyce and John Broadus.

In 1885, Mullins graduated from Southern Seminary, and his peers thought so much of him that they chose him to speak at the graduation ceremony. He delivered an address entitled "Manliness in the Ministry." He then took up his first pastorate in Harrodsburg, Kentucky. Before accepting the call, Mullins had wanted to become a missionary to Brazil. He had written to the Foreign Mission Board seeking an appointment, but he never received a response. In Harrodsburg, Mullins married Isla May Hawley and the couple had two sons. Both died in childhood.

In 1888, Mullins was called as pastor of the Lee Street Baptist Church in Baltimore, Maryland. He served this church for seven years. He then accepted a position as associate secretary of the Foreign Mission Board, but soon moved on to become pastor of Newton Centre Baptist Church in Boston. This church was identified with the northern Baptists, and was in close proximity to Newton Theological Institute, Harvard, and Boston University. Mullins thrived in the rich intellectual environment and loved his ministry in Boston. However, conflict in Louisville would soon propel him back to the South.

In Mullins' absence, his alma mater had been thrown into its second great theological crisis (behind the Toy controversy). The third president of Southern Seminary (behind Boyce and John Broadus) was William H. Whitsitt, who took office in 1895. In scholarly articles, Whitsitt argued (correctly) that Baptists emerged from seventeenth-century Puritanism. He thus rejected the commonly held view of Baptist historic successionism—that Baptists could trace their history all the way back to John the Baptist. However, his position created a firestorm of controversy, and in 1898, the seminary trustees accepted Whitsitt's resignation as president. In searching for a new president of the seminary, the trustees wanted someone untainted by the Whitsitt controversy. They turned to Mullins, who had been outside the mainstream of Southern Baptist life during his time in Baltimore and Boston. After receiving the seminary's invitation to become its fourth president, Mullins paid a visit to Louisville to confer with the faculty and decide whether to accept the job. While there, he contracted an illness, and when he arrived back in Massachusetts, he collapsed into his wife's arms, almost in delirium from excessive fever, unable to speak. For weeks, Mullins was bedridden.

Finally, when he was out of danger, his wife asked him about the presidency of Southern Seminary. Mullins said with tears in his eyes, "The task is mine—ours." They wept together.[34] In 1899, Mullins took office as Southern Seminary's fourth president.

Under Mullins' leadership, the seminary grew in both enrollment and reputation. The faculty doubled in number. Mullins moved the school to a new campus. Mullins also became active in denominational life, becoming one of the SBC's most formative influences.

Mullins was a remarkably successful Baptist administrator. He served on the "Committee on Denominational Efficiency," which issued a report in 1914 urging the various boards and agencies of the denomination to remember "the unity of their common cause and the necessity of their cooperation with each other."[35] Out of this concern, in 1917, came the SBC Executive

Committee. Also, in 1925, under Mullins's leadership, the SBC launched its "Seventy-five Million Campaign," which resulted in the creation of the Cooperative Program. The Cooperative Program was and remains the lifeblood of Southern Baptist agency activities.

Mullins served as SBC president from 1921-1924. He was the primary architect of the 1925 Baptist Faith and Message. He was also instrumental in setting up the Baptist World Alliance as a worldwide fellowship of Baptists.

Mullins developed a serious illness after visiting Poland in 1927. He was too ill to attend that year's Southern Baptist Convention meeting, even though it was in Louisville, his hometown. Mullins died on November 23, 1928, and was buried in the seminary's burial ground.

Theologically, Mullins remains shrouded in controversy. It legitimately can be said of him that he represented both continuity with the past and, at the same time, a fundamental break from the past in Southern Baptist life.

On the one hand, as Mark Noll has commented, Mullins guided the SBC "in drafting a conservative confession in 1925 and steered it away from evolution."[36] Under his determined leadership, Southern Baptists avoided the painful divisions of the Modernist-Fundamentalist controversy. In the 1925 Baptist Faith and Message, the SBC remained true to its confessional heritage.

But, as Noll also notes, "Mullins...defined Christian life in terms of experience rather than doctrine, a move associated since the beginning of the nineteenth century with Friedrich Schleiermacher, who is often called the father of modern Protestant liberalism." This emphasis on experience is apparent even in Mullins' contribution to *The Fundamentals*, where he asserted that "Christian experience" is a bridge to philosophy and a "point of contact" with the specific philosophy of pragmatism.

Unfortunately, Mullins' emphasis on experience over doctrine led to later doctrinal decline in the Southern Baptist Convention. As current Southern Seminary president R. Albert Mohler has written, Mullins "set in motion a decisive change in the seminary's theological direction." Mullins' textbook, *Christian Religion in its Doctrinal Expression* "charted a course away from Boyce's theological system" of classical Calvinism.[37]

While pastoring in the north, Mullins had come into contact with the theology of Schleiermacher, the pragmatism of William James and the personalism of Borden Parker Bowne (a professor at Boston University). For Schleirmacher, the essence of theology was not the systematic presentation of revealed truth, but reflection upon religious experience. For James, the founder of pragmatism, truth and experience were inextricably linked. From Bowne, Mullins gained a critical appreciation for the centrality of the person as the starting point for theological understanding. (Under the old system, the starting point was, of course, God.) Mullins drew upon both James and Bowne in his *Fundamentals* article.

In fact, Mullins' entire theological system was under girded by an emphasis on religious experience. Mohler argues that "this shift from biblical revelation to religious experience as the starting point and critical principle for theology represented a revolution from the influence of James P. Boyce and Mullins' other teachers at Southern Seminary."[38] As Sean Michael Lucas has observed:

> Mullins met the challenge of modernism by arguing that Christians had an experience that science could not understand nor analyze. This experience of Christ [preceded] any real understanding of facts and even could transcend understanding.... In order to demonstrate the truth of various doctrines, one did not need intellectual proof; rather, one simply pointed to the reality of Christ in the soul. Doctrines such as the deity of Christ and the authority of the Scriptures were settled by Christian experience. For Mullins, experience of Jesus Christ preceded doctrinal understanding.[39]

Mullins did not seem to realize that his mediating pragmatism was an inherently unstable basis for religious authority and that it pointed toward theological relativism, since personal experience is diverse by its very nature. (Your experiences of life are different than mine, but we both have God as our point of contact.) He also did not seem to understand that personalism is dangerous, in that it denies the importance (if not the existence) of any truth not rooted in personality. Lucas has observed that Mullins' approach to apologetics involved significant concessions to modernism, which Mullins himself failed to recognize, but which were fleshed out by later Southern Baptist theologians.

This, however, did not make Mullins a theological liberal. Instead, Mullins sought to defend evangelical convictions against liberalism and modernism. He sought to build a bridge between the Reformed theology of the past and the modernism of his own day. But because of his reliance on religious experience, Mullins' theological system and his defense of the faith shared a common starting point with the modernists—the human self.

31

Mullins affirmed the inspiration and truthfulness of the Bible. However, he held to a dynamic model of inspiration rather than a plenary verbal one.[40] At the same time, however, he accepted a division between scientific and religious knowledge. To him, religious truth in the Bible is secured by divine revelation mediated through the experience of the biblical writers and mediated again through the religious experience of the reader. Thus, there was no claim of inspiration connected to what he saw as non-religious issues. This viewpoint of less-than-full inerrancy left Mullins free to negotiate during the years of the Fundamentalist-Modernist controversy.[41]

For example, Mullins never declared himself on the issue of evolution. During the Scopes trial, he refused to help either William Jennings Bryan or Clarence Darrow, despite requests for assistance from both sides. Mullins vehemently denied to representatives of Darrow that he was an evolutionist. Nevertheless, both Albert Mohler and David Dockery believe Mullins secretly affirmed "some sort of theistic evolution," but "only to the extent that such a position would not threaten the supernatural element in the Bible, nor identify him as an evolutionist."[42] Mullins strongly defended the supernaturalism of the Bible, but he resisted those who wanted the SBC to take an official stance on evolution.

Mullins told the 1922 Southern Baptist Convention:

> "First, we will not tolerate in our denominational schools any departure from the great fundamentals of the faith in the name of science falsely so-called. Second, we will not be unjust to our teachers, nor curtail unduly their God-given right to investigate truth in the realm of science. Firm faith and free research is our noble Baptist ideal. Third, we will be loyal to every fact which is established in any realm of research, just as we are loyal to the supreme fact of Christ, His virgin birth, His sinless life, His atoning death, His resurrection and present reign."[43]

Mullins' vacillation and lack of precision of language (some say purposeful) on these critical issues permitted both conservatives and moderates in the 1980s SBC inerrancy debate to claim him as an ally. The problem was that both parties could marshal support for their claim from Mullins' writings.

Given his general theological stance, it should come as no surprise to learn that Mullins adopted a mediating position with respect to the doctrines of grace. Regarding election, he argued that God chose certain persons for salvation because of their potential influence upon other persons. Yet he continued to advocate election and expressly denied that our election is based on

God's foreknowledge of an individual's response of faith. On the other hand, he rejected limited atonement and irresistible grace. Mullins thus rejected and at the same time reinterpreted the Reformed heritage of the Southern Baptist founders and his former professors Boyce and Broadus. Mullins' mixed position on the doctrines of grace led to a rejection of those doctrines by his successors. In 1978, Herschel Hobbs sought to draw on Mullins' legacy by revising Mullins' *The Axioms of Religion*. In the revised edition, Hobbs undoubtedly spoke for many in declaring:

> God's purpose in election is to save not a few but as many as possible. Frank Stagg says, "One is strangely insensitive to the throb and pulse beat of the whole New Testament if he thinks that each man's fate is determined for him in advance. This is not a 'rigged' television show. God is not playing with toys or manipulating gadgets; he is seeking men who stand in awesome freedom where they may accept or reject the salvation which God alone can offer....
>
> God's foreknowledge as to those who would or would not believe does not mean that he caused it. He offered every incentive for man to believe. The final choice lay with man. God in his sovereignty set the condition. Man in his free will determined the result.[44]

Mullins' focus on experience also led him to focus on something he called "soul competency." This was interpreted by Mullins to mean that each individual person is independently competent to determine matters of religious importance. He claimed that this notion defined Baptist identity. Moderates of a later day seized upon this idea of "soul competency" to suggest that their methods of interpreting the Bible were just as valid as the literalism of conservatives.

Mohler offers the following retrospective on the influence of Mullins upon the generations that followed him:

> The central thrust of E.Y. Mullins's theological legacy is his focus on individual experience. Whatever his intention, this massive methodological shift in theology set the stage for doctrinal ambiguity and theological minimalism. The compromise Mullins sought to forge in the 1920s was significantly altered by later generations, with personal truth inevitably gaining ground at the expense of revealed truth.
>
> Once the autonomous individual is made the central authority in matters of theology—a move made necessary by Mullins' emphasis on religious experience—the authority of Scripture becomes secondary at best,

regardless of what may be claimed in honor of Scripture's preeminence. Either personal experience will be submitted to revelation, or revelation will be submitted to personal experience. There is no escape from this theological dilemma, and every theologian must choose between these two methodological options. The full consequences of a shift in theological method may take generations to appear, but by the 1960s most Southern Baptists were aware of a growing theological divide within the denomination, and especially its seminaries....

Mullins's attempt to forge a mediating theological paradigm for Southern Baptists eventually failed because mediating positions are inherently unstable. Delicate compromises established in one generation are often abandoned in short order as new generations assume leadership.

The emphasis on soul competency is, as Mullins must have both hoped and expected, the most enduring element of Mullins's legacy. The concept does underscore the necessity of personal religious experience—including repentance and faith—to the Christian life. But soul competency also serves as an acid dissolving religious authority, congregationalism, confessionalism, and mutual theological accountability. This too, is part of Mullins's legacy. As American Baptist church historian Winthrop S. Hudson asserted: 'The practical effect of the stress upon soul competency as the cardinal doctrine of the Baptists was to make every man's hat his own church."[45]

The irony should not be lost that the modernism that Mullins fought so diligently to keep out of the front door of Southern Baptist life, he allowed in through the back door. (Indeed, modernist tendencies were already in the door at Southern Seminary during Mullins' tenure through the teaching of missions professor W. O. Carver.) Thus, Hudson's prediction has proven true: In today's Baptist circles, "every man's hat" is his own church. Mullins left Southern Baptists with a theological confusion that still saddles us today. As Lucas rightly comments, "For over seventy years, Southern Baptists have harvested the shallow discipleship and vapid theology that resulted from sowing Mullins' theological seeds of experience."

What is interesting is that both liberal/moderate Baptists and (for lack of a better phrase) conservative, non-Calvinistic Baptists reflect that theological confusion. For all their differences (which we do not minimize), the two perspectives are alike in that their theologies are inherently unstable. Liberalism runs by nature to an intellectual abandonment of the doctrinal content of the faith.

34

A conservative, non-Calvinistic system runs by nature to a practical ignoring of the doctrinal content of the faith. In the end, there is no difference. Perhaps we will see that, another generation or two down the line, conservative, non-Calvinistic Baptist theology will end up being virtually indistinguishable from liberal theology. As Charles H. Spurgeon recognized in his day, the downgrade always ends up in the same place.

Chapter Two

The Beginnings of Reformation in The Southern Baptist Convention

The Rise of the Founders Movement

The Reasons for Our Hope

In Chapter 2, we offered our diagnosis of the problem with American evangelicalism: It is sick and dying because it has abandoned its Calvinistic foundations. Our prescription for a cure is that our churches return to the old paths from whence they drifted.

We have reasons to hope for a full recovery.

In the first place, Calvinistic Christianity is nothing more and nothing less than biblical Christianity. It follows, then, that the future of Christianity itself is bound up in the fortunes of Calvinism. Obviously the future of Christianity itself is not in doubt, for our Lord declared that the gates of hell shall not prevail against God's church. And yet we should be quick to acknowledge, of course, that God is not obligated to keep his church existent in America. In God's sovereign providence, Christianity has been wiped out of other cultures over the centuries of its history. Still, we have hope for revival because our hope is in the God who revives. The same God who opened our own eyes can open the eyes of others.

In the second place, despite evangelicalism's turmoil, there remain true Christians present in America. Wherever true Christians exist, hope for revival must also exist. For whoever believes in God's redemption through Christ and recognizes his own utter dependence on God, whoever recognizes that salvation is of the Lord, whoever seeks to glorify God in his worship and life, that person is already implicitly a Calvinist, no matter what he calls himself. In such circumstances, to make the person an explicit Calvinist, all we are required to do (humanly speaking) is to show the believer the natural implications of these already-held fundamental principles, which underlie all true Christianity, and trust God to do his work, that is, trust God to reveal these implications to the person.

In the third place, across denomination boundaries, God has been pleased to open many formerly blinded eyes to the truth and light of the doctrines of grace. In these days, the old paths are being trodden afresh. Interest in the writings of the Puritans, the theology of Jonathan Edwards, and the preaching of Charles Spurgeon and Martyn Lloyd-Jones, has increased exponentially. Undoubtedly, access to historical and contemporary treatments of the doctrines of grace on the Internet has something to do with this. In the last ten years, at least, God has used the Internet to do more to bring exposure to historical reformed theology than anything else. It is not an exaggeration to say that for this generation, it represents what the Banner of Truth Trust was for the last—the vehicle by which mass exposure is brought to the teachings of

38

those spiritual giants who walked before us.

Narrowing the focus to our own Southern Baptist Convention, God has used mightily the work of the Founders Movement to bring about widespread exposure to and acceptance of the doctrines of grace. This chapter describes the rise of the Founders Movement. It endeavors to explain what we pray is only the beginning of the beginning of the beginning of a massive movement of God toward the glorious work of local church reformation.

The Starting Place

What is now known as the Founders Movement can be traced back to a simple idea in the mind of a single Florida pastor in the late 1970s. Ernest Reisinger[46] was the senior pastor of North Pompano Baptist Church, a small SBC church in North Pompano Beach, Florida. Reisinger did not think to begin a Southern Baptist reform movement. Instead, he had a much smaller vision in mind— to republish an old Baptist systematic theology and send a copy to every graduating Southern Baptist seminary student.

By God's providence, Reisinger was the right man in the right place at the right time. He had come to the ordained ministry late in life. For over twenty years, he had owned and operated a successful contracting business in Carlisle, Pennsylvania. There, he had also been a founding elder of Grace Baptist Church, which by the 1960s had become the flagship reformed Baptist church in America. Thus, Reisinger had long held to the doctrines of grace. In fact, he had been instrumental in leading many others in the broader evangelical world to appreciate and love these doctrines. Reisinger also understood the power of sound literature. He had served for a number of years as a trustee of the Banner of Truth Trust, the premier publishing house of reformed theology and Puritan reprints. Through his lay preaching ministry and other personal contacts, he had influenced countless numbers of men and women to discover for themselves the deeper truths of the doctrines of grace. Then, after retiring from the contracting business in 1966, Reisinger was ordained to the gospel ministry and served several churches in Pennsylvania and Florida. He had retired to Cape Coral, Florida, he thought for the last time, when, in 1976, God called him to his greatest work.

Reisinger was summoned out of retirement to rejuvenate a virtually lifeless North Pompano Baptist Church. He had begun a reform work there, and was beginning to see significant fruit in the congregation. Some of his work in that church is described in his own words in the next chapter.

Although busy with the local church reform work at North Pompano, Reisinger also longed for spiritual renewal and reformation in the Southern Baptist Convention as a whole. Reisinger had a deep love for the SBC. Although he was sometimes accused of not being a "real Southern Baptist" since he had spent a number of years in an independent Reformed Baptist church; this charge was inaccurate. Reisinger's baptism was in a Southern Baptist church and the first church he joined after his conversion was a Southern Baptist church (First Baptist of Havre de Grace, Maryland). Thus, Reisinger wanted to give something back to his home denomination. Frustrated with the liberal bent of the convention in the 1970s, he enlisted the support of his church to launch what he called the "Boyce Project."

The "Boyce Project" was to republish *Abstract of Systematic Theology* by James Petigru Boyce, the primary founder and first theology teacher of the first Southern Baptist seminary. The goal was to distribute Boyce's *Abstract* to every student graduating from the six official Southern Baptist seminaries and a few more.

Reisinger, his associate pastor Fred Malone, and the North Pompano church, began the Boyce Project for several reasons.

First, they believed the project would bear fruit for God in the whole Southern Baptist Convention. They believed that the Southern Baptist founding fathers had a grasp of God's truth which they longed to see taught and proclaimed in our day. They longed for the faith of our fathers, the Biblical faith that would strengthen evangelism and holiness in the Southern Baptist Convention.

Second, at the time they started the project, Reisinger could not, in good conscience, lead his church to give large sums of money to the Southern Baptist Convention's Cooperative Program. He believed that, in that time period, the convention was out of step with orthodoxy itself, not to mention the Reformed theology of James P. Boyce, so much so that he could not allow the church to contribute heavily to its causes. Theological liberalism was rampant in the convention's leadership and agencies, and the conservative resurgence that has now brought the convention back from the brink of ruin had not yet begun. Hence, he saw the project as "cooperating" in a different fashion—by contributing to the theological development of young ministerial students and exposing them to the doctrines of grace believed and loved by our Baptist forefathers.

Why Boyce? James Petigru Boyce was the leading founder for organized theological education in the Southern Baptist Convention. Born in 1827 to a wealthy South Carolina family, Boyce was converted during his college years at Brown University under the influence of Francis Wayland. Boyce received his theological education at Princeton Theological Seminary, under the sound tutelage of Archibald Alexander, James Alexander and Charles Hodge.

For a time, Boyce struggled with the issues of Calvinism, resenting the suggestion that the doctrine of election was a reflection of the goodness of God. One of his former students, David Ramsey, called this the deepest soul struggle that this young Charlestonian had in the formative period of his life. But Boyce met and conquered his enemies through faith, and the reward of victory shone forth in all his thinking and teaching.

His famous sermon, "Three Changes in Theological Education," his inaugural address as a professor at Furman University, sounded the clarion call for an educational emphasis in Southern Baptist life.

Along with Basil Manly and John Broadus, Boyce founded The Southern Baptist Theological Seminary, the SBC's mother seminary. He served as its first president and contributed much of his personal fortune to its continued existence at a time when its future was very much in doubt. Hence, even in the era when the convention had been captured by the liberal element, Boyce was revered as the founder of Southern Baptist theological education. As Roy Honeycutt (later president of Southern Seminary and no sympathizer to Calvinism) wrote in a 1979 letter to Reisinger, "We owe our existence as a seminary to [Boyce], and the entire Convention is indebted to him for the significant contribution he made in instituting theological education at the seminary level among Southern Baptists."

Boyce was not afraid to be found on the "old paths." His beliefs and his teaching were decidedly Calvinistic. He believed what his friend Charles Spurgeon said about that doctrine: "That doctrine which is called 'Calvinism' did not spring from Calvin; we believe that it sprang from the great founder of all truth. Perhaps Calvin himself derived it mainly from the writings of Augustine. Augustine obtained his views, without doubt, through the Holy Spirit of God, from the diligent study of the writings of Paul, and Paul received them of the Holy Ghost, from Jesus Christ, the great founder of the Christian dispensation."[47]

In the classroom, Boyce's earlier struggles with Calvinism made him sympathetic to the struggles of his students. Ramsey recalled: "Sometimes in the class discussions a Newfoundland fog would settle over us, but through the darkness there was ever one gleam of light; Boyce's face with his great blue eyes shining on. Memory wings its way back across the years. I see Dr. Boyce in the old Fourth Avenue lecture room the last day of the class, which was the last time I ever saw him. I left him there. Also I left many of my doubts and difficulties on the same spot. My religious life, I trust, has expanded, my creed grown shorter and deeper, but like the face of a young man whom I know whose characteristic features are practically the same as they were at two years of age, only grown more mature, so has my creed on Calvinism and free grace."[48] E.E. Folk also commented on Boyce: "He was a great teacher. He could get more hard, solid study out of a boy than any teacher whose classes we ever had the privilege of attending, with possibly one or two exceptions. You had to know your systematic theology, or you could recite it to Dr. Boyce. And though the young men were generally rank Arminians when they came to the seminary, few went through this course under him without being converted to his strong Calvinistic views."[49]

Boyce's legacy is the biblical theology expressed in the *Abstract of Systematic Theology*. Created from his classroom notes, the final revision was completed in 1887. Boyce never considered the *Abstract* to be a masterpiece for the learned, but he envisioned it as a practical textbook for students and pastors. The famed Princeton theologian B.B. Warfield said about Boyce's *Abstract*:

> In the selection and ordering of the matter, in the proportion of its distribution, and in the method of its presentation, the same fine judgment is displayed which has governed his theological conceptions themselves.... The result is that he has given us a textbook which we are glad to place on the same shelf with ours Drs. A.A. Hodge, Dabney, and Smith, and with his Dr. Strong, as another admirable compend of Augustinian theology.[50]

Reisinger and Malone wrote a publisher's introduction to the reprint of *Abstract of Systematic Theology*, in which they made a strong appeal for the theology of Boyce and the founding fathers of Southern Seminary. The following extract from the introduction provides a flavor of Boyce's character:

> *Boyce's Christian Character*
> There are several incidents which related how Boyce's character as a man and a Christian gave great weight to his influence and teaching.
> During one of John Broadus' illnesses, Boyce personally paid for a trip for him to get rest. Arriving at the hotel, Broadus was too ill to climb the stairs to his room. Dr. Boyce then lifted his colleague into his arms and bodily carried him to his room. Broadus said, "He seemed strong like a giant, and he was tender as a woman." Such was his manhood....

42

One of the highest tributes was paid to Dr. Boyce when a student returned to Southern after several years interval. When asked why he returned, he said, "I want to attend Systematic Theology and hear Dr. Boyce pray." There cannot be a greater complement to a teacher of theology....

Boyce's Legacy and Message Today

Dr. Boyce founded the first Southern Baptist Seminary in 1859 along with John A. Broadus, Basil Manly, Jr. and William Williams. At its founding the seminary rang out a theological clarity that we pray this reprinted *Abstract of Systematic Theology* will help preserve and ring out still to the present generation. This is the faith of our Baptist fathers which we believe is still the Biblical faith for their children. May God grant it a thorough reading today.

Boyce was reared in a Calvinistic atmosphere and also immersed in the doctrines of grace that dominated Princeton Theological Seminary where he entered as a student in 1849. At Princeton, he was taught and influenced by some of the leading theologians such as Charles Hodge and Archibald [Alexander]....

Boyce's close friend and fellow founder of the seminary, John A. Broadus, expressed his own feelings about the theology of Boyce which we call Calvinism: "It was a great privilege to be directed and up borne by such a teacher in studying that exalted system of Pauline truth which is technically called Calvinism, which compels an earnest student to profound thinking, and when pursued with a combination of systematic thought and fervent experience, makes him at home among the most inspiring and ennobling views of God and the universe He has made."

....The board of trustees, in its first meeting after Dr. Boyce's home going, expressed their sense of deep loss, calling him "the father of the great institution over which he presided. Identified with it from the beginning, he gave the whole of his noble life to it. Without his sagacious counsels, his heroic exertions and his sublime self-sacrifice, the institution could not have survived its trials. The seminary is his monument, and a blessed memorial to him is written in the hearts of the people of God." What a fitting tribute this was to one who said, "The seminary is my child."

His life's teaching was the theology of John Bunyan, Charles Haddon Spurgeon, George Whitefield (the greatest evangelist that ever put foot on American soil), Jonathan Edwards, William Carey and Adoniram Judson, great Baptist missionaries. Boyce had such a

43

respect for Charles Spurgeon that he visited him in England during the last year of his life in 1888. His daughter records that Spurgeon asked Dr. Boyce to speak at his Pastor's College, but he declined. She said that her father literally trembled and became short of breath because of being in Spurgeon's presence. Such was his love and respect of Spurgeon, that after the meeting he told his daughter, "Compared to him, I have done nothing."

Dr. Boyce's legacy to us and to our posterity is the biblical theology expressed in the *Abstract of Systematic Theology*, which is nothing other than his classroom teaching.... According to Mueller, he always considered it not to be a masterpiece for the learned but a practical textbook for students and pastors without seminary training. This is its great value for today, profound enough for the seminarian, simple enough for the layman...

As a theologian Dr. Boyce is not afraid to be found 'in the old paths.' He is conservative, and eminently Scriptural. He treats with great fairness those whose views upon various points discussed he declines to accept, yet in his own teaching is decidedly Calvinistic, after the model of 'the old divines.' Difficulties as connected with such doctrines as the federal headship of Adam, election and the atonement he aims to meet, not so as to silence the controversialist, but so as to help the honest inquirer. (Quoting The Standard of Chicago).[52]

In their introduction to the republished work, Reisinger and Malone expressed their prayerful desire that Boyce's *Abstract* would obtain a wide distribution and that its reading would provide a catalyst for change in Southern Baptist pulpits and pews. Their hope was that a discovery of the theology of Boyce would cause pastors and leaders to change the man-centered evangelism so characteristic of our day to the God-centered evangelism of Boyce and the founders. They fervently believed this was the greatest need in twentieth-century evangelism:

Many a life has been changed by one book. And we want to say again, that the views that Boyce taught are not some strange, new theological opinion that comes racing on the contemporary scene, but it is that of our first founding fathers; the founding fathers of the first Southern Baptist Seminary....

And we long to see those doctrines that Boyce taught, that our founding fathers believed, that Spurgeon, Bunyan, George Whitefield and Jonathan

Edwards preached, we long to see those truths thunder through America and through our Baptist churches. This is our desire; this is our motive; this is our longing prayer that God would be pleased to own this work to the glory of His great and holy name, and to the good of His church.[53]

Publishing the Boyce volume required massive effort and sacrifice by the small North Pompano church. Reisinger and the den Dulk Foundation planned and proposed the project. However, it was the church members that carried it. Many in the congregation made a real financial sacrifice to fund the project. Elderly ladies would purchase one book each month from their social security checks to give to a seminary student.

After the Boyce volumes were reprinted, Reisinger wrote to the six presidents of the Southern Baptist seminaries asking permission to visit their campuses and present the book to graduating students. At some seminaries, he spoke in the chapel service.

In the 1978-1979 school year alone, the North Pompano Baptist Church distributed over 2,000 copies of Boyce's Abstract of Systematic Theology. By the end of 1980, the church had distributed over 5,000 copies of Boyce's book, and Reisinger and Malone had received hundreds of encouraging letters from the graduates who received them. They continued the project in 1981, giving away over 1500 copies that year. All in all, the church ended up republishing and distributing over 12,000 copies of the *Abstract of Systematic Theology*.

As Reisinger and Malone distributed Boyce volumes, they wrote to each seminary graduate who received a copy of Boyce's Abstract:

> I am writing this letter to take a little survey of opinions on a few of the chapters in Boyce's *Abstract of Systematic Theology*. For your cooperation in this survey, we will send you a free copy of the Old Baptist Confession of 1689, later adopted by the Philadelphia Association out of which the Southern Baptists came.
>
> The questions:
> Do you believe that Dr. Boyce is biblically correct in his chapter on Effectual Calling (Chapter XXI—page 367)?
> Do you think his view of the Doctrine of Election is the biblical teaching (Chapter XXIX—page 341)?
> In Chapter XXVIII - page 295, Dr. Boyce sets forth several views of the Atonement. Which view do you believe to be the biblical view?

45

Reisinger never dreamed that the Boyce Project would become the unlikely spark that God used to ignite a fire of reformation in a number of Southern Baptist churches. Through the distribution of Boyce's *Abstract*, the reformation fire was spread from pastor to pastor, member to member, one person at a time. It was God who opened the eyes of those who truly saw for the first time. This is illustrated by the following letter, written by Don Whitney, a student at Southwestern Baptist Seminary in 1979 and now a professor at Midwestern Baptist Seminary and leader in the Founders' Movement:

> Late in April 1979, I was walking through the Student Center at Southwestern Baptist Theological Seminary in Ft. Worth, TX. A man with a box of books at his feet asked if I were graduating next month. When I told him I was, he offered a copy of the book, provided I simply read a few specific pages and responded in writing to the sheet of accompanying questions. I paused, knowing that I wouldn't have time to complete that assignment during the last week of school, but finally agreed on the condition that I could fulfill their request in a few weeks. Later that day, back in my apartment in Irving, I placed my new copy of James P. Boyce's systematic theology on a bookshelf. I can still see it pulled halfway out of the shelf, my self-reminder to keep my word about the reading and responding.
>
> Sometime during the summer I found the time to take down the book and read the section selected for me. Out of sheer obligation I finished the pages and dutifully wrote my answers to the questions. The heart of my response was: "Thank you for the book. But Boyce's views in this passage cannot be true, for if he is right then there's no such thing as free will. ("And," I implied, "everyone knows that we all have a free will.")
>
> In January of 1980 I assumed my first pastorate, a country church near Arkadelphia, AR. Shortly thereafter I began preaching through the book of John in the morning and Ephesians in the evening. By the time I got to Ephesians 1:4 I had to deal with the subject of election. I decided to check everything I could find in my library on the subject. I remember locating twenty-nine different sources which dealt with the issue, from commentaries to systematic theologies, including the book by Boyce. As I read, a change began to come over my thinking. Previously I had believed that the doctrine of election was either true or false. Now I realized that was a false dichotomy. EVERY

ONE I read believed that the Bible taught election, they simply differed on what it taught. It dawned upon me that, after all, "election" is a Bible word, not a word developed by theologians.

My second encounter with Boyce was read with new eyes. This confrontation with the Scriptures on the subject, and the arguments of men such as Spurgeon and Boyce, shattered my preconceived ideas about and prejudices against the sweet doctrine of God's sovereignty in choosing whom He will to salvation.

For the first time in my life I think I understood grace. I thought back to my conversion at age nine. When I was six I had a long illness which could have killed me, and was nearly run over by a car at age seven. I realized that had not the Lord spared my life, and then drawn me to Himself, I would have been at that moment a young boy in Hell and deserving to be there. Previously I would have thought as many do (though no one would be crass enough to say it) that, "Yes, the Lord saved me, but at least I had enough sense to know what to do when I heard the Gospel." Now I realized that I had contributed nothing to my salvation but my sin, and that God had no obligation to save me or even to allow me to hear the Gospel. I had nothing to offer Him, no claim upon Him. He saved me purely out of His sweet sovereign grace and mercy.

I put my head down on my desk that February morning in 1981, and sobbed convulsively over my sin, presumption, foolishness, and the wondrous, free grace of God.

Another Southern Baptist theologian also recognized the importance of the Boyce Project and the part it played in re-introducing Calvinism to Southern Baptist life. In 1982, Dr. James Leo Garrett told a class of students at Southwestern Seminary:

Now, I want today...to introduce some sub-types of Southern Baptist Theology. There are some movements that seem to be on the horizon....Now, I call these sub-types because I am assuming (this may be a faulty assumption), but I am assuming that not one of these can really claim to be the majority belief of all 13 million Southern Baptists...these are minority movements, or they are sub-categories; they are movements or they are teachings that have surfaced in Southern Baptist life enough that you can see them and detect them, but you may not know where they are going from here.

Dr. Garrett went on to discuss five movements within the Convention: (1) the Charismatic Movement; (2) Dispensationalism; (3) the Biblical Inerrancy Movement; (4) The Keswick Movement; (5) the Calvinistic Movement. This is what Dr. Garrett had to say about our Baptist Calvinistic roots:

> Fifth: The Calvinistic Movement. Now, this is a movement that asserts the truth and the viability of the strong Calvinism that we can find in our Southern Baptist past and our English past. It is an affirmation of strong Calvinism that we can find in our Southern Baptist past and our English Baptist past. It is in a sense an effort to recapture the Calvinism that has been lost in the last three quarters of the century, or so, and to cover this involves a new emphasis on the writings of John L. Dagg and James P. Boyce and of the 1644 and 1689 Particular Baptist Confessions of Faith. The North Pompano Baptist Church in Pompano Beach, Florida, of which Ernest Reisinger is the pastor, now offers to give a copy of James P. Boyce *Abstract Of Systematic Theology* to every graduate of the six Southern Baptist Convention Seminaries and to Mid-America and Luther Rice Seminary graduates. So, when you graduate here, all you have to do is go by and sign your name and you'll get a free copy of Boyce, thanks to the North Pompano Baptist Church of Pompano Beach, Florida.
>
> Now, I would like to say that there is one difference that I can see between the neo-Calvinist movement and the other four. You may want to disagree with this, and that's all right. I believe that it differs from the other four in that it can more widely claim endemic to the Baptist past, the Baptist heritage and teachings of the past, than can the other four. What I am saying is that whether we want to be Calvinists or not, today, any serious study of our Baptist past must acknowledge that Baptists have been Calvinists. To distort that is to distort the records, it seems to me. So what I am saying is that: it seems to me that the neo-Calvinist movement is able to say, "we are recovering part of our Baptist past" in a way that the charismatic movement cannot say, because the charismatic movement represents something that is not endemic to the Baptist past, that has not been a common practice in Baptist churches through the years, and not been a teaching that has prevailed....[I]t is not a part of the Baptist past the way the Calvinistic doctrine is. So I think I can draw that one distinction and be relatively fair in that assessment, and that dispensationalism as well is not endemic to the Baptist past in the same way that this new Reformed or Calvinistic [is]. I don't mean to

48

suggest by that, that therefore it is valid and the other four not, in some kind of sweeping statement. I am simply making that observation.[54]

As he traveled to the various Southern Baptist seminaries presenting Boyce's Abstract to students, Reisinger was permitted to speak in chapel only at New Orleans Seminary and Golden Gate Seminary. Although speaking to students in chapel at Southern, Southeastern and Southwestern seminaries was out of the question, the Boyce Project, at least initially, received a warm reception from the presidents of those institutions—men who were on the other side of the inerrancy controversy. For example, Russell Dilday, then-president of Southwestern Baptist Seminary, wrote to Reisinger:

> Thank you again for what your church is doing in helping seminary students get acquainted with some of the classical books of theological expression. I have particularly enjoyed the David M. Ramsey's Founders Day address at Southern on Dr. Boyce. Thank you for your interest and help. Our students certainly appreciate the generous gift.
>
> Cordially,
> Russell Dilday

This warm reception soon cooled, however, as the seminary presidents began to understand the nature of Boyce's theology. One student told Reisinger that, as a result of the Boyce book, "You can hear discussions of Calvinism in the parking lot." Dilday soon barred Reisinger from distributing Boyce's Abstract on the Southwestern campus.

In contrast, Paige Patterson, then-president of Criswell College, received the book warmly. He not only graciously offered to distribute the book during graduation exercises, held as part of the regular Sunday evening worship service of First Baptist Church of Dallas, which guaranteed the book exposure to 30,000 to 40,000 people (including radio audience), but he also invited Reisinger to speak at a chapel service and ensured that the book was sold through the Criswell Center bookstore on a regular basis. George Davis, chairman of the chapel committee, took some books with him to distribute on mission trips to rural parts of the country.

Patterson had a deep appreciation for the history of the Southern Baptist Convention. He wrote his dissertation on John L. Dagg and, at Reisinger's request, wrote the following introduction to the reprint of Dagg's *Manual of Theology*:

Periodically, the work of a seminal thinker who influenced his own generation will burst, like a long dormant volcano, upon another generation with renewed vitality. The present treatise on theology by John Leadley Dagg was pivotal among Baptists in the South in its own era. Dagg's works represented the first full system of theology prepared by a Baptist in America, including monographs on theology, ecclesiology, ethics, and apologetics. The sociological ferment of the Civil War and reconstruction periods produced an eclipse of the work of this former president of Mercer University in Georgia.

In a day when many are searching for their 'roots,' Baptists need to rediscover their own heritage. For this reason, many will greet the republication of Dagg's theology and ecclesiology as the harbinger of a new day. If one wishes to know what most Baptists believed during the formative days of the Southern Baptist Convention, he will discover it in this volume. With remarkable insight, John Leadley Dagg—pastor, theologian, evangelist, teacher and college president—presents the essay of biblical truth in a thoroughly readable, yet scholarly presentation.

The indefatigable spirit of this early Baptist thinker, who suffered numerous physical reversals, glows with experiential insight into the crucial doctrines honored by Baptists everywhere. Every pastor, professor, and seminary student should avail himself of the opportunity to become acquainted with one of the most sublime of our Baptist fathers.[55]

Although Patterson obviously admired Dagg, it soon become obvious to Reisinger that Patterson did not hold to Dagg's theology. Reisinger wrote Patterson on May 5, 1981:

Paige, as you know, I am with you 100% on the battle of inerrancy. However, my concern goes one step farther, that is, What does this infallible Bible say? What does this infallible Bible mean, that is, what does it teach?—and, How does it apply to those to whom I preach?

They had several vigorous exchanges on the extent of the atonement. On September 10, 1981, Patterson wrote:

It would be inappropriate and dishonest for me to deny that Dr. [Tom] Nettles and Ernest Reisinger are more Calvinistically turned than I am. You would be correct in your assumption that I would reject the concept of a limited atonement as it is most frequently defined in

Calvinistic theology, and would even want to be sure I heard the definitions on three others of the traditional points of Calvinism. However, if the two poles under consideration are Calvinism and Arminianism, I am certainly far more Calvinistic than anything else. As your letter would indicate, you doubtless have found the seat of my reticence about much of contemporary Calvinism, i.e., its tendency to foster a stifling of world missions and evangelism. Of course, I am not so naive as to believe the two are necessary concomitants, only that they have too frequently found a home together.

...I am just grateful to God that those of us who do have a thorough belief in the sovereignty of God, unshakable confidence that salvation is all of God's grace, and a quiet confidence that God has revealed Himself propositionally through the pages of the Bible as well as in a living way through Christ are able to get along together victoriously even when we may be somewhat at odds in some of the details. I would hope that process would continue.

...There has never been the slightest feeling on our part that you nor Dr. Nettles nor any of the other precious saints of the Lord that we know in our Baptist fellowship are anything other than compassionate and industrious in your search for the souls of lost men. Consequently, you are always welcome here and, in fact, we desire your fellowship and presence.

On February 17, 1982, he wrote:

It is apparent that we differ some in regard to soteriological matters—at least regarding the order of events in soteriology. What does concern me even more greatly, however, is that we are going to eventually forfeit the Southern Baptist Convention as a forum for the discussion of differences among people who have no questions about the total truthfulness of the Bible unless we stay together. I see the possibility of a rift developing between Bible-believing conservatives over the question of the extent of the commitments to Calvinistic theology. If we allow the rift to take place at this stage of the game, I am convinced that it could be all the detractors of the Bible need to wreck our effort to establish the source of truth among Baptists.

I am certain that you have no more desire to see this happen than I, but I want us always to keep before us the importance of staying together until we can win this primary battle concerning the authority of the Word of God.

Some years later, on August 21, 1995, Patterson, by this time president of Southeastern Baptist Theological Seminary, reiterated in correspondence to Reisinger that "the liberals would love to see a division among us and are actively promoting it....Let's be sure we don't give them an opening."

Reisinger heartily agreed that conservatives had to stay together to stave off the liberals in the Convention. He repeatedly told Paige Patterson, Adrian Rogers, Paul Pressler and other leaders of the conservative resurgence that the Calvinists in the convention identified with and supported the conservatives in the inerrancy battle. He recognized that the liberals would have loved to see a division among conservatives, and he was determined not to allow that to happen. Tom Nettles, professor of church history at Southern Baptist Seminary, and Timothy George, dean of the Beeson Divinity School of Samford University, likewise stated that they would hate to see those who hold common views on the nature of the biblical revelation censure one another over the differing views of grace. After all, if the whole house is on fire, what good is there in arguing over which room one should sit in?

At the same time, there could be no mistaking an overtone of hostility against Calvinism on the part of some conservative leaders. Paige Patterson had these words to say about John Calvin in a May 10, 1982 letter to Reisinger:

> I deeply resent ever being called by the name of a man who baptized babies, thought he found the Church in the Old Testament, and thought nothing of his failure to rescue Servetus from the flames when a word from him would have been sufficient."

He explained that his strong words stemmed from his belief that acceptance of the doctrines of grace lead to apathy toward evangelism:

> We have severe difficulties with some of the student disciples of the Calvinists that we do have on the faculty [of Criswell College] who now eschew evangelism and, in two cases, have even left Baptist churches to go into 'covenant congregations.' I will not be party to anything that seeks to deter our young preachers from the stated task of reaching the 4 billion people on the face of the globe with the gospel."

Reisinger responded on May 20, 1982 with the mild statement that "all true Christians are Calvinists on their knees." He told Patterson that "the only people who do not believe in limited atonement in its application are Universalists." He again responded on June 16, 1982, graciously acknowledging that a combination of heavenly zeal, true piety and sound doctrine, joined with biblical evangelism, such as that seen in Calvinists Bunyan, Spurgeon, Whitefield, and Edwards was "rare upon the earth." He confided that the marriage of a Calvinist foundation and a zeal for evangelism was "the burden of my life."

The Founders' Movement

The Boyce Project had in immediate impact beyond the seminaries. For example, it inspired Bob Selph, pastor of the Miller Valley Baptist Church of Prescott, Arizona, to distribute a small book he had written, *Southern Baptists and the Doctrine of Election*, to all Southern Baptist pastors. This book had a positive impact on many pastors' views of Calvinism. Unfortunately, the Yavapai Baptist Association did not see it the same way. It formally charged Selph with heresy for his agreement with the historic Southern Baptist view of unconditional election. He was subjected to formal proceedings that stopped short of removing him and his church from the association. Thankfully, in 1993, the same association adopted a resolution repenting of this sin against Selph and his church.

The greatest immediate impact of the Boyce Project was in the many new contacts Reisinger made as a result of his travels distributing Boyce volumes to seminary graduates. As more and more Southern Baptists began to understand, appreciate, embrace and love the truths of the doctrines of grace, Reisinger and Malone received letters and telephone calls from hundreds of young Southern Baptist pastors wanting help in applying those precious doctrines to the Christian life and to church practice.

The following letter from a pastor in Cascilla, Mississippi is representative:

> I came to embrace in my early years as a Christian some of the truths of the "doctrines of grace," and have attempted, especially since entering the pastorate about a year ago, to implement these theological understandings into the work of evangelism. I find myself the pastor of a rural church in Mississippi which is basically untheological in its approach to Christianity and church order and practice. Of course, when there is a dwarfed under

standing of the doctrines of the Bible, there is a consequent shrinking of the spiritual life of the church members. I must also confess that I, as the pastor, am not completely clear in my own mind as to the proper approach on the practical level to evangelism and church order. I am well versed in the "decisionizing process"...and am dissatisfied with its fruits, but am not ready to discard the invitation system completely. My problem is that I have never seen a church which embraces the work of evangelism and has instituted church order from this biblical standpoint while remaining fervent and experiential in its outworkings of the Christian life.

...Could you help me? How do you lead folks to a conversion experience without "decisionizing" them? Applying the emphasis you speak of on teaching, when and how do you lead the sinner to close with Christ? Realizing that baptism is the biblical way of confessing Christ as savior and of identifying with him, how does a church accept a person as being a proper candidate for baptism? How do you do this in a congregation which would consider discarding the invitation system as heresy and has such a low view of conversion and regeneration and no concept of biblical church order? Could you make an attempt at answering some of these? I realize that some of them are matters of practicality, but I am a bit perplexed as to how to proceed.

This letter added a P.S.: "Do you know of any churches and pastors in this area which are concerned with reformation in the local church which I could have fellowship with?

Heart-felt concerns like this, spurred on by the rediscovery of books like Boyce's *Abstract*, led a group of men concerned with restoring the doctrines of grace and their practical implications to Baptist life to form the Southern Baptist Founders Ministries.

It started during Reisinger's spring 1979 visit to Southwestern Seminary to distribute Boyce books. He stayed in a campus dorm, and one night, struck up a conversation with the switchboard operator. The operator was a student who told Reisinger that the best professor on campus was Dr. Tom Nettles. Reisinger had already heard about Nettles from another student, and so he made it a point to meet him. Reisinger and Nettles quickly discovered that they were like-minded on the doctrines of grace. They also discovered that they both had a deep concern to fellowship with other Southern Baptist Calvinists and encourage one another that they were not alone—that others existed who shared their convictions. They began to pray together, crying out to God for wisdom and direction to satisfy the need they saw for fellowship among Southern Baptist Calvinists.

Meanwhile, Reisinger began to gather from his personal contacts and voluminous correspondence the names of Southern Baptist pastors who were at least sympathetic to the doctrines of grace. By July 1982, he was busy making contact with an informal network of over 500 Southern Baptist preachers, by mail or phone, at least twice a month, to discuss their mutual interest in the theology of Southern Baptist fathers such as Boyce, Broadus, Dagg and Mell. On October 6, 1982, Reisinger sent the following letter to pastors who shared an interest in reformation in the denomination:

> This is a form letter and I am sorry I do not have time to write a personal letter at this time. However, I would really appreciate your cooperation.
>
> There are an increasing number of men among Southern Baptists who have come to a knowledge of those great truths of our founding fathers. John A. Broadus, in describing the theology of Dr. James P. Boyce, called these truths "that exalted system of Pauline truth which is technically called Calvinism." I have quite a few names and there must be many more.
>
> Several persons have expressed a desire that we compile a mailing list of such men within the Southern Baptist Convention. The immediate purpose would be that we could have some contact with each other and possibly recommend such men to churches in our various associations that are without a pastor. Also, we could recommend the men and their churches to our own people who are vacationing, or moving and seeking a church that holds to the biblical beliefs of our Baptist fathers.
>
> Secondly, we may be able to have a little newsletter every three or four months to keep in touch with each other. Definitely not to form an organization or party, but principally for acquaintance and fellowship.
>
> Your name has been given to me by a mutual friend so I am writing this letter to ask if you would send me the names and addresses of men in the Southern Baptist Convention that you know who believe the Doctrines of Grace, or are sympathetic toward these Doctrines. For this assistance, I will send you the list of names when it is compiled.

I am enclosing a copy of our church paper, "Good News." If you would like to be on our mailing list for subsequent copies, please advise.

With warm Christian regards,
Sincerely yours in Christ's service according to my light and power,

Ernest C. Reisinger.

Then, on November 13, 1982, Reisinger, Nettles and Malone met at a Holiday Inn in Euless, Texas, for prayer to seek God's direction with respect to a Southern Baptist conference ministry. Nettles brought to the meeting several young men who had embraced the doctrines of grace. Among them were Bill and Tom Ascol, Ben Mitchell and evangelist R.F. Gates. Reisinger later called this one of the most meaningful prayer meetings in which he had ever participated. The attendees spent the first half of the day in prayer, reading Psalms and hymns. During the second half of the day, they discussed ideas. They finally settled on the idea of a conference with the doctrines of grace as its foundation. Thus began the Southern Baptist Founders Conference.

The Founders Conference

The group decided that the purpose of the Founders Conference would be to promote instruction in both doctrine and devotion, as expressed in the doctrines of grace, and the experiential application of those doctrines to the local church, particularly in the areas of worship and witness. This was to be accomplished through the putting on of conferences where a variety of speakers would be engaged to present formal papers, sermons, expositions, and devotions, and at which literature consistent with the nature of the conference would be recommended and sold.

The motive was to provide encouragement to Southern Baptists through historical, biblical, theological, practical, and ecumenical studies that would glorify God, honor his gospel, and strengthen his churches. To this end, the group agreed that the theological foundation of the conferences would be the doctrines of grace, those doctrines known as the five points of Calvinism (e.g., total depravity, election, atonement, effectual calling, and perseverance) and related truths. These subjects would all be presented doctrinally, expositionally, homiletically, and historically. Each conference would concentrate on the experiential and pastoral application of the respective doctrines.

With fear and trembling the first conference was planned and held August 1-4, 1983, on the campus of Southwestern University (now Rhodes College) in Memphis Tennessee. The speakers and topics were:

> Pilgrim's Progress & Teaching Grace – James D. Gables
> Life & Labors of P H Mell – Ben Mitchell
> Sovereign Grace in Romans 8 – Richard P. Belcher
> Sovereign Grace in Romans 9 – Richard P. Belcher
> The Doctrine of Election – J.W. Baker
> Doctrines of Grace In Baptist History – Tom Nettles
> Doctrines of Grace In Church Planting – George McDearmon
> Doctrine and Devotion – Ernie Reisinger
> Lordship of Christ – David Miller
> The Effective Call – James Millikin

The Founders Conferences have continued annually ever since. Until 1991, they were held at Rhodes College. Since 1991, the conferences have been located at Samford University, in Birmingham, Alabama. Speakers have included such distinguished men of God as John MacArthur, J. I. Packer, John Piper, Al Mohler, David Dockery, Timothy George, Tom Nettles, Walter Chantry, Al Martin, Iain Murray, Errol Hulse, Ligon Duncan and Geoff Thomas. These and other speakers have impacted countless numbers of attendees, as demonstrated by the following letter published in the fall 1992 issue of The Founders Journal:

> This letter is written to you to express my sincere appreciation for your hard work and dedication to the furtherance of the gospel through a Southern Baptist conference that promotes the faith of our founders. While I realize this gathering is primarily for pastors, I feel it is something through which all believers can derive great benefit. I want to express some of the benefits I have received:
>
> As this is my second year to attend the conference, I arrived with a spirit of anticipation that I would be greatly blessed as I had been in the prior year. Not to my surprise I came away with a feeling of rejoicing in my heart, a renewed mind, and an uplifted soul. I can truly say with the Psalmist, "O Lord, our Lord, how excellent is thy name in all the earth!" Time after time, the men of God ushered me into the throne room and I worshipped at His feet. What a marvelous blessing!

While I ponder and contemplate the messages at hand, I find myself falling on my knees and crying out..."Search me, O God, and know my heart: try me, and know my thoughts: and see if there be any wicked way in me, and lead me in the way everlasting." I examine myself and find there to be many wicked ways within me. Praise His name that He is a merciful and forgiving God!

Although my soul has been thrilled, my heart is weighted down with the heaviest of burdens and feels as if it would at any moment break into a thousand pieces as I think of all the lost and dying souls in the world! It seems too great a task, an overwhelming mission—nevertheless, my Lord has commanded me to go, and that is what I must do. The time spent last week has reinforced this in my mind and heart. O that I would be a faithful servant to do His will!

It seems an incredible and amazing thing to think that just a year ago I was living in darkness without even a will to go on living! Yet today I sit here writing to you having seen the brilliant splendor of the Lord Jesus Christ. Truly the Lord is my light and my salvation without whom there would be no hope. It is my greatest desire to share the joy of this light with others. Your endeavors this past week have been mighty in the promotion of the Kingdom of God. I will use my experiences to implore others to come and hear the proclamation of God's word.

Finally, I am writing this letter to encourage you in the faith, to be strong and not to grow weary in well doing. We, as the flock, must realize that our shepherds do become discouraged and weary at times. I will lift your name before the Lord that He would give you strength, wisdom and boldness in your labors on behalf of Him.

L. G.

From its humble beginnings, the Founders Conferences have continually grown. In 1999, almost 600 ministers, students and interested lay people attended the conference in Birmingham, Alabama and heard John Piper give an unforgettable series of messages on fulfilling the Great Commission by becoming missionary martyrs. About the same number heard Ligon Duncan speak movingly on God's sovereign providence the next year.

Founders Ministries

From the conferences came a ministry designed to channel

and guide the resurgence of the doctrines of grace in the convention. It is now called Founders Ministries. In 1987, Founders Ministries formed its first youth conference. As of the time of this writing, Bill Ascol has organized and led this conference, and acted as camp manager and camp chaplain, for twelve years. Moreover, numerous regional conferences more or less affiliated with Founders Ministries have been held on an annual basis all around the United States.

In 1990, the decision was made to begin publishing a quarterly journal, *Founders Journal*, under the editorial direction of Dr. Thomas K. Ascol, pastor of Grace Baptist Church in Cape Coral, Florida. In the inaugural issue, Dr. Ascol explained the reason for the journal:

> This journal, as the name reflects, emerges out of the same concerns and principles which have guided the Southern Baptist Conference on the Faith of the Founders over the last eight years. The energy which is being generated by the divine renewal of the Doctrines of Grace among Southern Baptists should be conserved and guided. The *Founders Journal* hopes to be of use in this effort by providing historical, biblical, theological, practical, and ecumenical studies which will glorify God, honor His gospel, and strengthen His churches....
>
> The plan is to publish a quarterly journal with articles which reflect doctrinal and devotional commitment to the Doctrines of Grace (election, depravity, atonement, effectual calling, and perseverance) and their experimental application to the local church. Contemporary voices, as well as those who "being dead, yet speaketh," will be featured. Sermons, expositions, essays, letters, book reviews and newsworthy notes will be included.[56]

Ascol continued to expound the reason for Founders Ministries' existence in the second issue of *Founders Journal*:

> No blind adherence to tradition motivates this desire to return to the faith of our founders. Nor is there any incipient desire to canonize our "Baptist fathers." Rather...God's truth does not change. If what these men believed was true then, it is still true today. If they were correct in their understanding of the gospel, then it is incumbent upon us to have our own beliefs accord with theirs. If they were incorrect, then we ought to repudiate their views and renounce a significant part of this denomination's heritage. The question is open to debate, and should be addressed on the basis of what God's Word teaches.

The first two issues were distributed free of charge. There would be no further issues unless a sufficient number of readers demonstrated an interest in continuing the publication. Fortunately, they did. Ascol wrote in the second issue: "Cards and letters which have been received indicate that the initial issue of the *Founders Journal* has met with a warm welcome among ministers and laymen from across the country. A pastor in Valdosta, Georgia writes, 'God bless your work. It is desperately needed!' His sentiments were echoed by many...."[57] The Founders Journal began with about 200 subscribers in 1991. As of 1999, it was distributed to over 1200 readers. In 1995, a special SBC Sesquicentennial Issue of Founders Journal was published and sent to every pastor, missionary, and professor in the Southern Baptist Convention.

A pastor from Palo Pinto, Texas commends the first issue of the journal as "a fine balance of irenic polemics and devotional edification." This is precisely the spirit and balance which we hope to promote. We are not so naive as to believe that every Southern Baptist will join with us in returning to our theological heritage. Reasonable men who love the Lord and who desire to know His will occasionally differ in their interpretation of various biblical teachings. This has ever been the case. Where such honest disagreement exists, Christian charity should be extended while seeking to establish the biblical arguments for one's views. This journal intends to reflect such a spirit as it contends for the doctrines of grace.

Public Opposition

While the *Founders Journal* may be "a fine balance of irenic polemics and devotional edification," as suggested in the above-quoted letter, the opponents of the doctrines of grace have not always been so charitable in their descriptions of Southern Baptist Calvinism.

For example, William R. Estep, professor of church history emeritus, Southwestern Baptist Theological Seminary, leveled a sweeping broadside against Ernest Reisinger (by name) and other Southern Baptist proponents of Calvinism in an article published in the Texas Baptist Standard, March 26, 1997. He accused Southern Baptist Calvinists of having "only a slight knowledge of Calvin or his system" and of "simply borrow[ing] that which they assume to be both biblical and baptistic without adequate research." He contended that the Calvinistic system is "without biblical support." It arrogantly assumes "to know more about God and the eternal decrees upon which it is based than God has chosen to reveal in scripture or in Christ." Its advocates worship a God who "resembles Allah, the god of Islam, more than the God of grace and redeeming love revealed in Jesus Christ." Its view of human responsibility makes "a person into a puppet on a string or a robot programmed from birth." It is "anti-missionary." Its proponents historically have been "marked by intolerance and a haughty spirit." In sum, according to Estep, "if the Calvinizing of Southern Baptists continues unabated, we are in danger of becoming 'a perfect dunghill' in American society."[58]

Tom Ascol responded in the next edition of *Founders Journal*:

> Dr. Estep's article seriously misrepresents what John A. Broadus called "that exalted system of Pauline truth which is technically called Calvinism." I am sorry that it appeared in its current form. The topic which he addresses is an important one and should be discussed. But such discussion ought to conducted on a high level, working diligently not to misrepresent those with whom we disagree, seeking not only to be understood but to understand, and with renewed commitment to love the brethren—even those, perhaps I should say especially those, who differ with us theologically.[59]

Albert Mohler, president of Southern Baptist Theological Seminary, also responded that if Calvinism were accurately represented by Dr. Estep's treatment, he would have nothing to do with it. "Nevertheless," he continued, "few of Calvin's friends or enemies will recognize Calvinism as presented in Estep's article."[60] He went on to correct Estep's portrayal of Calvinism.

Roger Nicole answered Estep in the form of a "Dear Colleague" letter, responding in devastating detail to Estep's misrepresentations of Calvin's own teachings, concluding with the observation: "I do find comfort in the thought that although you may oppose Calvinism on this earth, you will be yourself a Calvinist when you get to heaven, for I say 'Who will deny or seek to restrict the sovereignty of God when appearing before His throne?'"[61]

Mark Wingfield, then-editor of Kentucky Baptists' *Western Recorder*, also took aim at Southern Baptist Calvinism in a September 9, 1997 editorial, declaring that the doctrine of particular redemption "drives a dagger through the heart of the gospel" and "doesn't breed a natural zeal for missions." In an attack apparently directed at Southern Seminary and Albert Mohler's presidency, he opined that just because the SBC's founders believed in the doctrine, that did not make it right. "Many supported slavery, for example, and believed women should not have the right to vote."

Thom S. Rainer, dean of Southern Seminary's Billy Graham School of Missions, responded sharply: "I simply cannot let your inaccuracies and innuendoes pass without comment...Your editorial is hurtful, inaccurate and divisive." He continued: I can say without fear of inaccuracy that the emphasis on missions and evangelism has increased exponentially since Dr. Mohler came as president."[62]

As these attacks reveal, much of the opposition to the revival of the doctrines of grace in Southern Baptist life has consisted of essentially unsubstantiated name-calling and clumsy *ad hominem* barbs. Curiously, the opposition has never really attempted to mount a biblical defense of the non-Calvinistic position. One could speculate that this is because liberals who do not hold to the full authority of Scripture drive much of the vitriol. Perhaps their goal is more political than theological—that is, as Patterson pointed out, to drive a wedge through the conservative coalition now in charge of the convention.

Recognizing this aspiration on the part of the liberals, some prominent conservative Southern Baptist leaders have been more muted lately in their statements about Calvinism. Despite his antipathy toward the full Calvinistic position, as discussed above, former SBC president and current Southeastern Seminary president Paige Patterson stated in November, 1999: "There's plenty of room under the [SBC] umbrella for anyone who is anything from a one- to five-point Calvinist. There's room for a two- or three-pointer like me, provided he can explain what is meant by two and three. There's room for four- and five-pointers whom I believe lack scriptural justification for that, but I'm certainly not in favor of running them out."[63] Indeed, when *World Magazine* suggested that Patterson and Mohler had "locked horns" on the issue of Calvinism in the convention, the two seminary presidents wrote a joint letter to *World* stating that they had "never really discussed the subject," although they "intuitively know that we do not see the order of salvation events and some aspects of election exactly the same."[64]

While Patterson has been somewhat circumspect in his comments, Adrian Rogers has not been so guarded. In correspondence, sermons and pamphlets, he has represented Baptist Calvinists as believing that God does not love everyone and that he condemns infants to hell. He has represented the doctrine of irresistible grace as teaching that God is "going to zap you...no matter what." He has referred to Calvinists as the "chosen frozen, the elite, the satisfied, the cheese and wine theologians." On March 13, 2000, he preached a radio message in which he called a belief in election and irresistible grace a "libel against God." He accused Ernest Reisinger in correspondence of having "more zeal for the cause of Calvinism than for missions and evangelism." He equated the God of Calvinism to the god of Islam and stated, "I refuse[] to let my church be dampened down by a form of incipient fatalism."[65]

Texas evangelist Freddie Gage has also stated that "there is not a nickel's worth of difference between liberalism, five-point Calvinism and dead ortho-doxy" because all are "enemies of soul-winning."[66] Of course, Edwards, Whitefield, Spurgeon, Carey and Judson would have been mightily surprised to learn that they were "enemies of soul-winning"!

Yet to be fair, if the criticism of opponents has, at times, been less than judicious, the zeal of converts to the doctrines of grace has been, at times, equally misplaced. Patterson and Rogers both have expressly linked their condemnation of the doctrines of grace to what they perceive to be the over-abundant zeal of Calvinistic men they have known. Frankly speaking, many who have sought to bring about reformation in their local churches have not gone about it in the right way. Sometimes their timing was wrong. Sometimes their methods have been wrong. Sometimes they needed the wisdom from above, described in the Epistle of James:"But the wisdom that comes from heaven is first of all pure; then peace-loving, considerate, submissive, full of mercy and good fruit, impartial and sincere" James 3:17 (NIV).

Some have caused unnecessary divisions over secondary matters (like eschatology). Others have not understood the biblical doctrine of accommodation (discussed in the next chapter). We all need more of the application of the words of our mentor, the great Apostle Paul, "And a servant of the Lord must not quarrel but be gentle to all, able to teach, patient, in humility correcting those who are in opposition, if God perhaps will grant them repentance, so that they may know the truth, and that they may come to their senses and escape the snare of the devil, having been taken captive by him to do his will" (2 Tim. 2:24-26 (NKJ)).

Recent Developments

Despite the misguided opposition of some and the misplaced zeal of others, interest in the doctrines of grace continues to grow apace among Southern Baptists. Founders Ministries has branched into the publishing business with the creation of Founders Press. And, with the explosive growth in the World-Wide Web as a means of publishing, Founders Ministries decided to go online in Winter 1996 to make the journal and conference information more widely available. Founders Ministries' web page, Founders Online, is found at www.founders.org. Founders Ministries' most recent venture is to assist like-minded pastors and lay leaders in local communities to join together for fellowship and encouragement through the formation of "Founders Fraternals."

Founders Ministries has recently received some attention in the broader evangelical world. Both *Christianity Today* and *WORLD Magazine* have run stories on it and the impact it has had in helping Southern Baptists discover anew our Calvinistic roots.

Calvinistic Southern Baptist churches continue to spring up all over the convention. Many of them are sponsoring their own web sites, which promulgate Calvinistic Baptist views more widely.

The primary goal of Founders Ministries is to assist and encourage preachers like the man who wrote the following letter published in the Summer 1997 *Founders Journal*:

> Dear Friends:
>
> I deeply appreciate the Founders Journal and its commitment to returning Southern Baptists to their historical theological roots. I have enclosed [a gift] to help with your ministry. Within the last couple of years, the Lord has given me a small degree of boldness to proclaim the doctrines of grace. I am beginning to sense what I am sure many of you dear brethren know all too well—that although the doctrines of grace are precious to us, they are hated and despised by others. I ask that you please pray for me. I have not experienced any open hostility, but I often feel faint. The Arminianism that we see both in and outside of the Southern Baptist Convention seems almost like a taunting Goliath that threatens to devour anyone who dares to challenge it. There is comfort, however, in knowing that, unlike David who had to fight alone, you brothers are out there. May the Lord bless and multiply your ministry.
>
> In Christ,
> T. H., Mississippi

And so the work goes on.

The Southern Baptist reformation started with a small stream as Ernest Reisinger planned and implemented his Boyce Project. By God's providential direction, the stream turned into a river with the formation and success of Founders Ministries. The river has now turned into a torrent as Southern Baptists all over America and beyond are beginning to rediscover, or discover for the first time, the reformed, Calvinistic roots of our denomination. A quiet revolution is slowly but surely spreading as God continues to open Southern Baptist eyes to the glorious truths of his grace. Only God knows how far it will go.

CHAPTER THREE

Walking Without Slipping

Instructions for Local Church Reformation

He will not let your foot slip—
he who watches over you will not slumber;
indeed, he who watches over Israel
will neither slumber nor sleep.

Ps 121:3-4

The Purpose of this Chapter

Some who read this small book are in the middle of or soon will be in a reforming situation. It is my goal in this chapter to encourage the reformation now going on, and impart some of the things I have learned over the course of my life and ministry.[66]

The first part of this chapter describes my own involvement in reforming one local church. I do not write as an authority on the subject of reformation, but I do write out of many years of experience in reforming situations. The years of experience have also included many mistakes. Experience is a queer old teacher. She first gives you the test and then the lesson. The principles discussed in this chapter are ones I've learned the hard way. Hopefully, recounting these things will spare some unnecessary shipwrecks in your local churches.

The second part of the chapter describes several essential principles applicable to reforming a local church. You should know that I have no blueprint or navigation map to offer. Each situation has different obstacles to deal with. The size of the church and the make up of the staff will impact the approach that should be taken, as will the kind of membership and the spiritual caliber of the leadership. I wish I could give you ten rules to guarantee success in reforming a church, but it is never that simple. There are no ironclad rules. This is because reformation is God's work. God uses human instruments as his means, but the determination of whether and when reformation fire falls is up to God. Therefore, the task to which we are called is to continue to work and pray. Perhaps God will open others' eyes even as he has already opened our own.

An Example of Local Church Reformation

Although God has been pleased to permit me to be involved in several reforming churches during my days of service, there is no question that my greatest challenge occurred at North Pompano Baptist Church in North Pompano Beach, Florida. When I arrived, the church had been without a pastor for a year. Before they called me, they had gone through 35 applicants!

I preached my trial sermon in June 1977, and I had no idea what I was getting into. If I had known the alarming problems facing that church, I would never have even considered the call. Now, of course, I am glad I did not know the problems, and I am certainly glad that I did accept the call. Looking back, I can say that it was a very providential call. The problems that existed at North Pompano Baptist were no different than the problems that exist in many, many

Southern Baptist churches. In a way, North Pompano was a micro-cosm of the modern-day Southern Baptist Convention.

I was the fifth pastor at North Pompano Baptist, and I was there for eight years, much longer than any of the four previous pastors. Yet my time there was not easy. Far from it. I soon dis-covered that the church was teetering on the edge of disaster.

For starters, I quickly recognized that the paid staff was far too large for a church of its size. We had about 900 people on the membership roll. Yet the paid staff included two church secre-taries, a paid pianist, a paid song leader, a full-time custodian, six to eight paid day-care teachers, another paid custodian for the day care, and a paid cook for the day care. Two weeks after I arrived, the electric company called to say it was coming to turn off the power because the electric bills had not been paid. The church was delinquent on its bills, while at the same time giving $13,000 a year to the Southern Baptist Convention Cooperative Program. In my view, this was sinful.

Next, the bank administering the church's $75,000 bond issue notified me that it would no longer service the debt because the church was continually late in making payments, and the bank was fed up with complaints from unpaid bondholders. This was an extremely serious matter. It would not have been easy to find another bank in our area to service the bond issue, since only banks large enough to have trust departments are qualified to handle such matters.

To make matters worse, we soon discovered that the financial secretary was embezzling money from the church. This cost the church at least $23,000 and likely more that we could not docu-ment. As a result of the acute financial crisis in the church, there was always pressure put upon me by church leaders to have what they called a "make-up Sunday." This meant taking a special offering for the purpose of making up what was needed to pay the bills. The church's financial situation wore on me. It was a major crisis and one I did not bargain for. God did not call me to be a fund-raiser but to preach the gospel. Nevertheless, I was in the middle of the mess, whether I had bargained for it or not. I did not know at the time that the church's spiritual problems were much worse than its financial picture.

Soon after arriving, I called two knowledgeable church leaders into my office to go over the 900 names on the church member-ship roll. We already knew that the church's finances were in shambles. We soon discovered that only about 110 people were carrying the financial load of the church. More importantly, we learned that the spiritual condition of the church was vastly more appalling.

One by one, we went through the names on the membership roll. I put an "R" (for regular) beside the names of all who attended church regularly (at least once a week). I put an "0" (for occasional) beside the names of those who attended occasionally (once a month). I put a "D" (for delinquent) beside the names of all those members we were positively sure had not attended, or even communicated with the church, for a year or more. This exercise was most revealing and very sad. Of the 900 members on the church roll, North Pompano Baptist Church had over 550 delinquents—people that I had never seen on the church premises, or even heard of, and most of whom could not be found. On a good day, only about 250 members bothered to show up for Sunday morning services. Only a handful attended Sunday night services, and only about twelve to fifteen attended the midweek prayer meeting. This examination revealed how false a picture of the health of the church the membership roll really was. If a business had falsified its records like this, its chief executive officer would have been sent to prison for fraud. This sad picture was the fruit of shallow man-made and man-centered evangelism.

Things only got worse. It soon became obvious that six of the twelve deacons gave no evidence of conversion. The remaining deacons were spiritually and doctrinally illiterate. They simply did not know what it meant to be and act like a Christian. Most of the membership was in the same sad condition. Sunday school teachers were living in open adultery. After I had been at the church only a short time, one deacon's wife commented, "This preacher thinks the only thing we do right around here is sin." She was not far from wrong.

The spiritual condition of the church members put me into a state of shock and dismay. My thoughts were full of only questions—with no answers that I could see. What could I do? What needed to be done first? How could I go about it, whatever it was? Where should I begin? I had no book of ten easy steps to solve these deep-rooted spiritual problems. Moreover, even if there were such a book, I knew it would not help. There were some things I simply could not do.

I knew that I could not change hearts, but God could. I could not give spiritual life, but God could. I could not open their understanding, but God could. I could not give an effectual call, but God could. I could not make them see the truths of the Bible, but God could. I could not reveal Christ to their hearts, but God could.

Oh, how I thank God for the "buts" in the Bible. We were by nature children of wrath; "but God, who is rich in mercy, because of His great love with which He loved us, even when we were dead in trespasses, made us alive together with Christ" (Eph. 2:4; NKJV).

71

Only God could open Lydia's heart (Acts 16:14). Only God could reveal to Peter that Jesus was the Christ, the Son of the Living God (Mt. 16:13-17). Only God could change the hearts of the people at North Pompano Baptist Church.

I was certain that this church needed the same thing the discouraged disciples needed when they were on the way to Emmaus—Jesus "expounded to them in all the Scriptures the things concerning Himself" (Luke 24:27; NKJV)—but I was equally certain that they needed something more. "He opened their understanding that they might comprehend the Scriptures." (Luke 24:45; NKJV).

Only God could take the dust of this world from their eyes so that they could see beauty in Jesus. Only God could take the wax of this world from their ears so that they could savingly hear the good news of salvation. Only God could raise the spiritually dead.

This is what drove me to call on him to do what only he could do. "If you then, being evil, know how to give good gifts to your children, how much more will your heavenly Father give the Holy Spirit to those who ask Him?" (Luke 11:13; NKJV).

Only God could do what needed to be done.

And yet I knew that in most, if not all cases, God uses human means to accomplish his purposes. It is just as important for us to assert the true validity of the secondary agent, man, as it is to assert the final cause, God. I had often received much help and good instruction from the great apostle Paul's letters to the young preacher, Timothy, during dark times. So once again, I turned to read and re-read those inspired letters of 1 and 2 Timothy. This time, like never before, the following verses leapt from the pages of holy writ to my mind:

> And a servant of the Lord must not quarrel but be gentle to all, able to teach, patient, in humility correcting those who are in opposition, if God perhaps will grant them repentance, so that they may know the truth, and that they may come to their senses and escape the snare of the devil, having been taken captive by him to do his will. (2 Timothy 2:24-26; NKJV).

From these verses, I learned three things that were essential to know in order to minister in the helpless situation in which I found myself.

The first is the spiritual state of the unconverted. They were slaves to Satan, locked in his prison house, without a key to get out (v. 26). They were helpless, and hopelessly taken captive by Satan to do his will (v. 26). They were ignorant of truth; a point implied in the phrase "correcting those" (v. 25). This also is the reason the true servant of the Lord must be apt to teach" (v. 24).

The second thing I learned from this passage involved some much-needed instruction for my own heart in dealing with this appalling situation. I was reminded that the servant of the Lord must not be quarrelsome or a man of strife. I was reminded that the servant of the Lord must be able to teach truth which his own heart acknowledges. That is, he must have a personal knowledge of the truth.

I thirdly learned that I had to depend on God for results. The phrase "if God" in verse 25 is a condition. God may grant repentance. He also may not. Hence, the servant's hope is not in his theological understanding, nor in his preparation, nor in the subtlety of his wit or in the power of his persuasion. No! The servant's hope is in God. And not only is it absolutely necessary for the servant of the Lord to put his trust and hope in God, but he must also teach the unconverted that their only hope of getting out of Satan's prison house is in the God who has the keys and the power to turn the lock.

I placed these instructions from 2 Timothy on my desk where I could see and read them every day. I recommend these inspired instructions to every minister in a reforming situation.

After much prayer and analysis, I concluded that the basic need of the people of the church was a solid doctrinal foundation. North Pompano Baptist, like many others, had absolutely no doctrinal foundation. The people were doctrinally illiterate, and by the time I got there, the superficial superstructure that remained was falling apart.

This is not surprising, in retrospect. After all, any effort to be a practicing Christian without knowing what Christianity is all about will always fail. Indeed, to believe savingly in Christ involves first believing the right things about him. Faith involves understanding who he was—the virgin born Son of God. It involves understanding what he did—suffer vicariously on a Roman cross. It involves understanding why he died on that cross—because of a covenant with God the Father to redeem a company of sheep from every tribe, nation and tongue that no man can number.

In my eight years at North Pompano, I kept before me two churches. One was the "Ideal Church," which was conceived from scripture. If I had ignored this one, I would have settled for status quo. The other was the "Real Church," the one I faced every Sunday morning at 11:00 a.m. The joy was in seeing the "Real Church" move toward the "Ideal Church," at first in baby steps, but soon in giant leaps.

The first foundation stone was what I called the "School of Deacons." I met with the deacons, the leaders of the church, and their wives every week, one hour before the Sunday evening service. In one year, I took them through the old London Baptist Confession of 1689. This was a very significant and profitable beginning. Some dropped out and left the church, but about half of them finished. These men, and a few others, became my best supporters and helpers. Their experience with God had been better than their understanding of God.

The second foundation stone was laid when I preached 27 messages on the Beatitudes, leaning heavily on material from Dr. Martyn Lloyd-Jones's book, *Studies in the Sermon on the Mount*. I emphasized Christ's teachings on the composition of a true Christian.

The third foundation stone was laid when I set up a book table to expose the people to solid literature. This was very profitable.

The response to a renewed doctrinal teaching was as varied as the response in the Parable of the Sower. Some left the church. One casualty in particular was especially painful. David Clifton was one of the most respected men in the church. He had held every office in the church: chairman of the deacons, chairman of the pulpit committee, and chairman of the finance committee. We had grown to be very close friends. Hence, I was shocked beyond words when, on February 15, 1979, I received the following letter from Dave:

Dear Friends,

It is with very much searching of heart, Bible study, prayer and scientific research coupled with an air of sadness that I am persuaded to write this letter. My purpose is to 'be as honest and as open with you as I know how in expressing to you my present spiritual condition. This condition has caused me to conclude that I should resign as Deacon, Visitation Leader, Chairman of the Nominating Committee and as a church member.

My present spiritual condition has resulted from a gradual deterioration of faith in the authenticity of the Bible over the period of the last year. I have discussed my condition with Brother Ernie several times over the last six months and he has tried to help me. I appreciate very much his efforts, but a change in my condition has not been forthcoming. I have not discussed this with anyone else except my wife and I would rather not do so; since in the process I might be tempted to defend my position and in so doing might cause someone's faith to be affected. My greatest concern in this announcement is that it might adversely affect some of you. I hope this does not occur.

I want to make it clear that I do not 'believe that the doctrines being taught by Brother Ernie and Brother Fred [Malone, my associate pastor] are unbiblical. On the contrary, I believe they are teaching exactly what the bible teaches. My problem is not with the teachers but with the Bible.

I shall miss seeing each of you and I shall always consider you my friends.

I was very saddened by Dave's response, for I loved him very much. Others in the congregation wanted to get rid of the messenger. However, thank God, many repented and got right with God, although, of course, this did not happen in a weekend.

Today's Evangelism

My experience with unregenerate church members at North Pompano Baptist Church spurred me to write *Today's Evangelism* in 1982. That book had its roots in an unceasing burden to see biblical evangelism restored to the church and to see a proper relationship established between sound doctrine and true heavenly zeal in evangelism.

In thinking about the membership at North Pompano Baptist Church and many other churches I knew, I began to ask the following questions:

> What was the caliber of supposed converts?
>
> Was there evidence of a real conversion experience?
>
> Was there a real conversion experience?
>
> Had a supposed conversion led to new life in Christ, to new purpose for living, and to a new pathway of obedience to Christ?
>
> Were the supposed converts brought into a living relationship with the Son of God?
>
> Were the supposed converts led to worship God and serve him in the church?

75

I had become convinced that man-centered evangelism had brought disaster to the church in the form of an unregenerate, impure church membership. I was persuaded that the church desperately needed a return to God-centered evangelism. I wrote:

> I am making a plea for every sincere Christian to examine all personal evangelism and public evangelistic preaching by this clear, New Testament, God-centered evangelistic message. Many of our serious church leaders and members know that there is something wrong with most of the so-called "converts," but they do not seem to trace the problem to the message of evangelism. This is why they are forever rushing on the contemporary scene with some new method, while the real problem is the message (p. 30).

God-centered evangelism presents the law to the unconverted person. If the law is ignored or left out, the meaning of sin is lost. Man-centered evangelism eschews preaching the law. There is bright singing, humorous witticisms, entertaining anecdotes, high-pressure techniques, and commercialism, but there is also a studied omission of the dark background upon which the gospel can effectively shine forth.

God-centered evangelism presents the lordship of Christ as a vital part of the gospel message. Our churches would not be filled with so many who give no biblical evidence of conversion if more ministers and members presented the lordship of Christ as part of the evangelistic message.

God-centered evangelism preaches repentance as a vital element of the message. Where saving faith is found, repentance is sure to also be found. Where evangelical repentance exists, saving faith will also be found. Faith and repentance are distinct but inseparable. As Calvin said, "Now it ought to be a fact beyond controversy that repentance not only constantly follows faith, but is also born of faith.... surely no one can embrace the grace of the gospel without betaking himself from the errors of his past life into the right way, and applying his whole effort to the practice of repentance." He continued: "Can true repentance stand, apart from faith? Not at all. But even though they cannot be separated, they ought to be distinguished...repentance and faith, although they are held together by a permanent bond, required to be joined rather than confused."[67] Yet repentance is strangely absent from most of present-day evangelism. It is here that many poor lost church members are self-deceived. They have missed repentance and are as lost as lost can be.

God-centered evangelism recognizes and acknowledges the

absolute necessity of the effectual call of the Holy Spirit for a person to be saved. It knows to be true what the Bible clearly teaches in John 6:44, that no man can come to Christ unless the Father draws him. Man-centered evangelism, on the other hand, acts as if the success of the gospel is owing to the power of persuasion or the eloquence of the person preaching the gospel. It ascribes the saving response to the gospel to man's will. God-centered evangelism knows better. No preacher, regardless of his training, preparation, eloquence, subtlety of wit, or power of persuasion can regenerate one soul.

God-centered evangelism believes that election is an act of God, not the result of the choice of the elect, that this choice is of individuals, not classes, and that it is by the good pleasure of God and according to his eternal purpose. Man-centered evangelism believes that salvation of individuals is merely the result of their own choice and perseverance, that God's election is simply an election of a class, or that so far as the election of individuals is concerned, it was only as God foresaw faith on the part of the believing person.

God-centered evangelism stresses that faith is man's duty, but that it is not within his ability. Man-centered evangelism leads men to believe that they are saved by a decision.

In God-centered evangelism, follow-up of believers is not necessary—the sinner willingly becomes a follower. Man-centered evangelism, however, is forced to cajole and pamper and beg so-called "converts" to do what everyone who is born again will want to do and will do without calling them every week to remind them and coerce them to worship and serve the Lord in his church.

Most evangelism of this day is not only superficial, but also radically defective. It is utterly lacking a foundation on which to base an appeal for sinners to come to Christ. The church desperately needs a return to God-centered evangelism. When it does, problems like those I faced at North Pompano Baptist Church would be avoided.

Despite all the hardships and difficulties, we were able to praise God for blessing the work far above what we could ask or think. Attendance at the prayer meetings more than tripled. Attendance at the evening service doubled. The debt was paid off, and the mortgage burned. We sent sound Christian literature to 3200 Southern Baptist foreign missionaries and 2400 home missionaries. We arranged for the translation of Dagg's *Manual of Theology* into Portuguese. We distributed from the church book table thousands and thousands of books and pamphlets. We even started a mission church in the Palm Beach area.

Reformation is hard work. I think I aged ten years during the first year I was at North Pompano Baptist Church. Yet with God's grace, wisdom and patience, it can be done.

Principles of Local Church Reformation—The Need for Reformation Today

I now want to turn to several principles that are essential for local church reformation. I hope these principles will be clearer to you after reading of my own experience at North Pompano Baptist Church.

The first principle is to recognize the need for reformation. Both the Bible and history record how the people of God are continually in need of self-examination and reformation. But in every case of reformation, there must be a recognition of the need. This is the first step.

Scripture records many accounts of true reformation. Sometimes whole communities, and in a few cases, whole nations, have been affected by reformation. For example, Nehemiah had to be informed by Hanani that the walls of Jerusalem were broken down and the gates of the city were burned with fire. Nehemiah recognized the great need for reformation, as reflected in his prayer of confession:

> "O LORD, God of heaven, the great and awesome God, who keeps his covenant of love with those who love him and obey his commands, let your ear be attentive and your eyes open to hear the prayer your servant is praying before you day and night for your servants, the people of Israel. I confess the sins we Israelites, including myself and my father's house, have committed against you. We have acted very wickedly toward you. We have not obeyed the commands, decrees and laws you gave your servant Moses. (Neh 1:5-7 (NIV)).

Habakkuk saw the sad condition of Judah in his day. He asked God, "Why do you make me look at injustice? Why do you tolerate wrong? Destruction and violence are before me; there is strife, and conflict abounds. Therefore the law is paralyzed, and justice never prevails. The wicked hem in the righteous, so that justice is perverted." (Hab. 1:3-4;NIV). Habakkuk recognized the great need for reformation, and so he prayed: "O Lord, I have heard your speech and was afraid; O Lord, revive your work in the midst of the years! In the midst of the years make it known; in wrath remember mercy" (Hab. 3:2; NKJV). This verse shows us Habakkuk's fear. He was afraid. He heard an alarming voice that produced an appropriate prayer and serious plea. This verse also demonstrates the potent need for reformation—"in wrath, remember mercy."

The psalmists likewise saw the need for reformation. The sons of Korah pleaded in Psalm 85:4: "Restore us again, O God of our salvation" (NKJV). Three times in Psalm 80, Aseph cried out to the Lord: "Restore us, O God of hosts" (80:3, 7, 19; NKJV).

We could multiply texts and examples from almost every prophet in the Old Testament. In every case there was a recognition of the need for reform.

This is the starting place for us, too. Too many people in the church do not know the marks of a true church. Because they do not have a vision of what the church should look like, they see no need of reformation.

The discerning Christian, however, would not question the need for reformation. The fact that the church of today has little spiritual influence in the world is manifest. Mature and observant Christians recognize that there is no doctrinal foundation, no fixed objective standard of righteousness, because the moral law embodied in the Ten Commandments is missing from most churches. We should be more concerned than we are that the doctrinal foundations of the law have been removed or buried in powerless ritualism. For when the moral and doctrinal standards are removed, the church is swept along without a compass by every wind of change in a sea of confusion. The Bible asks the question: What can the righteous do if the foundations be removed? There is a desperate need for reformation in the church.

Our Lord's last words to the churches that needed to be reformed are found in His messages to the seven churches in Rev. 2 and 3. These final messages reflect his deep love and concern for his Church. These messages are rich in instruction, warning and comfort. These messages contain much that is very relevant for reforming churches on the contemporary scene. Many churches are sleeping the sleep of death. Some are sounder asleep than others. Some are like Laodicea—they think they have need of nothing, but in truth they are pitiful, poor, blind and naked. But the good news is that, despite the sad condition there are always some children of light living among the dead. When Jesus said to strengthen the things that remain, he knew that there were some that would remain and, hence, that could be strengthened.

My encouragement, then, to those of you in sleeping churches is this: Stay in the fight. As long as you are able, strengthen the things that remain.

The Kind of Man God Uses in Reformation

The second principle of reformation is that the man behind the pulpit must have a reformed life before the people in the pews can ever be expected to change. It has been said that the minister's life is the life of the ministry. This is certainly true when we speak of reformation. We can be sure that if there is no reformation in the pulpit, there will be no reformation in the pews.

What kind of man does God use as his instrument of reformation? By a careful look at reformations in the history of God's people, we can discover the kind of man God uses, and therefore, the kind of man God expects you to be.

First, the man God uses in reformation is deadly serious about God's Word and God's work. If you are going to engage in reformation work, you must feel within yourself the responsibility to be a steward of the mysteries of God.

Indeed, when we examine the churches that have come alive, we see that the men leading them lived, labored and preached earnestly about eternity to eternity-bound souls. Horatius Bonar was such a man. As Samuel Zwemer wrote in the 1950 introduction to Bonar's *Words to Winners of Souls*, the keynote of Bonar's counsel to ministers was urgency. This was well expressed in the third verse of his hymn, "Go Labor On, Spend and Be Spent:

> Go, labor on while it is day,
> The world's dark night is hastening on.
> Speed, speed thy work, cast sloth away –
> It is not thus that souls are won.

Reformation men are serious men. They are not religious politicians seeking to climb the denominational ladder. Rather, they are men who have their eyes lifted to heaven. Everything they do and say is marked by earnestness, not just religious excitement. As was said of Richard Baxter, "When he spoke of weighty soul concerns, you might find his very spirit drenched therein." They are genuine men who know that necessity was laid upon them. They feel the urgency and weight of the cause of the gospel that is entrusted to them. They throw their whole soul into the conflict. As Bunyan said about his own preaching, they preach what they smartingly did feel.

Second, at the same time, reformation men are bent on success. If you are going to engage in reformation work, you must strive to succeed. You must be a warrior who has set your heart on victory. You must fight with believing expectation of victory under the guidance of our great Captain. I am referring, of course, to spiritual success, not worldly success. And, spiritual success is not necessarily correlated to statistical growth. Spiritual success may be had with statistical growth or without it. The point is, when a man enters Christ's army, that is, the ministry, he must be bent on success in order to avoid being a traitor to Christ. As shepherds we cannot sit on the mountainside in the ease of the breeze, heedless to the straying, perishing, bleating flock; but rather, there must be a watching, guiding, guarding and feeding of the sheep committed to our care.

How does this emphasis on striving for success comport with the notion that, pursuant to God's sovereignty, success is the Lord's business? The reformation man must believe with all his heart what Jonathan Edwards put in his *Miscellanies* (#29):

> When [God] decrees diligence and industry, He decrees riches and prosperity; when He decrees prudence, He often decrees success; when He decrees striving, then often He decrees the obtaining of the Kingdom of Heaven; when He decrees the preaching of the Gospel, then He decrees the bringing home of souls to Christ; when He decrees good natural faculties, diligence, and good advantage of them, He decrees learning; when He decrees summer, then He decrees the growing of plants; when He decrees conformity to His Son, He decrees calling; and when He decrees will, He decrees justification; and when He decrees justification, He decrees everlasting glory. Thus all the decrees of God are harmonious.

Third, the man who leads a reformation must be a man of faith. He must believe there is a time of plowing and sowing as well as a time of reaping. In other words, the man of God must plow up the soil of tradition and misconceptions and biblical illiteracy and then sow the gospel of the grace of God, believing that in due season there will be reaping if we faint not, knowing that our labor in the Lord will not end up in vain, knowing that we will return, bringing our sheaves with us. If you want to engage in reformation work, you must plead with God for men and plead with men for God. Fix your eyes on God's promises and plead as did the psalmist: "Remember thy word unto thy servant, whereunto thou hast caused me to hope" (Psalm 119:49; KJV).

Fourth, the man God uses in reformation must have confidence in the Savior whose commission he bears. If you want to engage in reformation work, you must have confidence in the Holy Spirit's mighty power. You must have faith in his power to take the wax of this world from the ears of poor, deaf sinners, faith in his

81

power to open the eyes that are blinded by the dust of this world, and faith in the power of the gospel, knowing it will not return void (Is. 55:11). You must trust that the gospel is "the power of God for salvation" (Rom. 1:16; NIV). If you would see a church come alive, you must go forth with faith in the power of the gospel.

Fifth, the man God uses in reformation work must be a man who diligently works. Jonathan Edwards spent thirteen hours a day in his study, preparing for sermons. Martyn Lloyd-Jones accepted a heavy load of midweek preaching engagements all over England, but never neglected his duties at Westminster Chapel. George Whitefield, in 1750, preached every weekday morning at 6:00 and again at 6:00 in the evening. He preached three or four times each Sunday and twice a week at Lady Huntingdon's church. During this time, he also sometimes conducted funerals, performed weddings, counseled enquirers, and kept up a large correspondence.

Sad to say, the ministry is infested with preachers who do not adopt the same attitude. There are a lot of fruitless preachers who do not labor for eternity. Yet for reformation to flourish, there must be some bearing of the burden in the heat of the day. There must be some unwearied toil of body and soul. There must be some of what the great apostle Paul speaks: "in weariness and painfulness, in watchings often in hunger, and thirst, in fasting often, in cold, and nakedness." Your attitude must be that there is no time for levity, sloth, or pleasure, for you are laboring for eternity. If you want God to use you, keep your back to the world and your eyes on the goal. Do not become entangled with the affairs of this world, that they may please you who has been called to be a laborer in the vineyard.

Sixth, the man God uses in reformation must be patient. Remember what Paul told Timothy, the young preacher? The servant of the Lord must be patient (2 Tim. 2:24). James also tells us to be patient (James 5:7-11). There must be great patience in the work of reforming a church. There must be a willingness to labor long without seeing all the fruit that one desires. Sow...sow...sow...day after day. Teach...teach...teach...week after week. You simply cannot be soon weary in well doing. You must keep in mind the passage from James that says "Therefore be patient, brethren, until the coming of the Lord. See how the farmer waits for the precious fruit of the earth, waiting patiently for it until it receives the early and latter rain. You also be patient. Establish your hearts, for the coming of the Lord is at hand" (James 5:7-8 (NKJ)).

Many a good plan has been aborted by impatience. Many a good day of toil has been thrown away by it as well. Neither you nor any other man can ever force reformation of a church. Yes, there must be intense longing for success, but much patience must be joined to that intense longing.

Consider that William Carey labored seven years before he baptized his first convert. Adoniram Judson toiled in Burma seven years before he harvested one soul. Robert Morrison sowed seven years in China before he baptized one convert. Robert Moffet waited seven years to see the first evident moving of the Spirit in Africa. Henry Richards spent seven long years in the Congo before he saw his first convert. What were these faithful men doing while they were waiting for results? They were patiently working, laying foundations, and sowing heavenly seeds, focusing on future generations.

Seventh, the man God uses in reformation must seek wisdom. The Bible tells us if any one lacks wisdom, he should ask of God who gives to all men liberally (James 1:5). God not only promises to give wisdom, but He describes this wisdom that He liberally gives: "But the wisdom that is from above is first pure, then peaceable, gentle, willing to yield, full of mercy and good fruits, without partiality and without hypocrisy" (James 3:17; NKJV).

Eighth, the man God uses in reformation must be bold and determined. Many who are Calvinists at heart are Arminians from the pulpit, and the reason is fear. But timidity shuts many a door of usefulness and loses many precious opportunities. Timidity wins no friends, while it strengthens the enemy.

Perhaps there was never an age where wickedness assumed a bolder attitude. Therefore, Christian boldness and courage is all the more required in reforming a church. Men must be strong and of good courage (Acts 4:13, 29, 31). We must adopt the attitude of Whitefield. When the vicar closed the church door, the evangelist preached in the churchyard!

Ninth, the man God uses in reformation is a man of prayer. Augustine said, "He that loveth little prayeth little, and he that loveth much prayeth much." Richard Hooker said, "Prayer is the first thing wherewith a righteous life beginneth, and the last wherewith it doth end." Bunyan said, "If thou art not a praying person, thou art not a Christian."

Prayer is essential. Many labor long and study much—but pray little. We often hear requests to "pray for the work." Oh, my friend, I am convinced that prayer is the work! Take the attitude of Hudson Taylor, the great missionary to China, who arose each night at 2:00 a.m. and prayed until 4:00 a.m. because he found it difficult during the day to have uninterrupted prayer. William

Grimshaw similarly had it as his custom to rise early in the morning, at 5:00 a.m. in winter and 4:00 a.m. in the summer, to begin his day with God. George Whitefield often rose from his bed in the night to intercede for perishing souls.

How, then, will your church attain to reformation? The answer is: By God's pouring out his sovereign grace upon the people of God. By using human instruments (a) who are deadly serious about the Word of God and the work of God, (b) who are bent on success, (c) who plow and sow in faith, hope and love, (d) who labor and bear the burden and heat of the day, (e) who have much patience, and (f) who spend time alone with God in prayer. Reformation is possible only through the outpouring of the Holy Spirit. But take heart. Luke 11:13 says, "If ye then, being evil, know how to give good gifts unto your children; how much more shall your heavenly Father give the Holy Spirit to them that ask him?" (KJV).

John Knox, in his old age, was helped into the pulpit by friends, but when he arose to preach, the Spirit of God's love burned in his heart in such a fashion that an attendant said, "So mighty was he in his yearning that I thought he would break the pulpit in bits." Oh, for some men with a deep yearning for God and for souls!

Laying a Foundation

The third principle of reforming a local church involves both the demolition of misguided theological notions and the laying of a biblical foundation anchored by the doctrines of grace.

It is impossible to over emphasize the importance of sound doctrine in the Christian life. Right thinking about spiritual matters is imperative if we are to have right living. As men do not gather grapes of thorns, nor figs of thistles, so sound Christian character does not grow out of unsound doctrine. J. C. Ryle once said, "You can talk about Christian experience all you wish, but without doctrinal roots it is like cut flowers stuck in the ground—it will wither and die." To put it another way: the devotional house must be built on a doctrinal foundation.

Biblical doctrine is more important than most church members realize. Doctrine not only expresses our experiences and beliefs, but it also determines our direction. It shapes our lives and churches. It gives our churches unity and stability. The church that neglects to teach sound biblical doctrine weakens the church membership. It works against true unity, invites instability in its fellowship, lessens conviction, and stalemates true progress in the church.

Unfortunately, however, we live in a church age where the doctrinal foundations of contemporary evangelicalism have crumbled and been destroyed. But God is interested in laying anew biblical foundations for future generations. He calls patient, persevering workers who long for reformation and who seek his wisdom to lay solid, doctrinal foundations!

Study Paul's epistles to the Romans, Galatians or Ephesians, and you will see that he always laid a doctrinal foundation before moving to practical subjects. If a church is to be reformed and come alive, there must be a doctrinal foundation. I believe we are in a reformation period of history. Many will be called upon by God to lay foundations of reform in churches. At the same time, in other churches, the foundations are being removed.

By contrast, the superficial man will think only of the "big show." He will not be concerned about how it comes about. He is only concerned with the superstructure. His concern is: Does it work? It is not: Is it true? But God is concerned about foundations, not superstructures.

We live in a day of quick, cheap, slick and frothy foundations, and our churches are reaping the sad, pitiful, painful, pathetic results. Our churches are full of carnal men who are not interested in being in the foundation-building business. Carnal men are not concerned with leaving a spiritual legacy for future generations. The only men who are interested in constructing a true foundation are those who have their eyes fixed on eternity. Foundation work is costly. It is painful. It is laborious. It is not showy. Who wants to watch concrete being poured into a footing? Foundation work is hard, dirty work.

Yet God Himself was into foundation work. He began His creative work by laying a foundation. As the psalmist said, "Of old hast thou laid the foundation of the earth" '(Ps. 102:25; KJV). Isaiah also declared of God, "My hand also hath laid the foundation of the earth" (Isa. 48:13; KJV).

What doctrines are we talking about? The doctrines that are worth dying for are foundational, biblical doctrines, not secondary ones. They are the doctrines believed in and preached by our Baptist fathers—men such as James P. Boyce, John A. Broadus, B.H. Carroll, John L. Dagg, Luther Rice, P.H. Mell, John Bunyan, Charles H. Spurgeon, William Carey, and Andrew Fuller.

We speak first of all of the doctrines of grace. Teach your people that they are utterly depraved and dead in their sins without God. Teach them that God chose the elect for salvation from the foundation of time out of his own mercy and desire, and that Christ died as a propitiation for his people. Teach them that it is the Holy Spirit who effectively calls sinners to salvation. Teach them that no one who has been converted can ever, for any reason, lose his salvation, but that true believers will persevere until the end.

In these doctrines we have a powerful message that is meant for today! We proclaim a powerful God who actually saves. Not a "little god" who can do no more than to help man save himself. Not a puny god who pleads with sinners to come to him and stands by helplessly, wringing his hands, while man makes up his mind.

We proclaim a faith that is utterly and completely God-centered. Our God is the source and end of everything that is, both in nature and in grace. He is sovereign in creation, sovereign in redemption, and sovereign in providence. History is nothing less than the outworking of God's preordained plan.

A prominent leader in the Southern Baptist Convention recently said that God does not overcome man's ability to resist God's grace. Our Baptist forefathers would not have agreed. They affirmed, as we do, that the Spirit's work involves more than mere enlightenment. It is a regenerating work in sinful man. In regeneration, the Holy Spirit takes away man's heart of stone and gives him a heart of flesh, renewing his will, causing him to come to Christ—not against his will, but freely, being made willing by God's grace. "Blessed is the man whom thou choosest, and causest to approach unto thee, that he may dwell in thy courts: we shall be satisfied with the goodness of thy house, even of thy holy temple" (Ps. 65:4).

The same Baptist leader who publicly denied irresistible grace also denied that God's redemption is particular to those God chooses to save. Yet just as the Holy Spirit of Calvinism is a Spirit whose calling cannot be resisted, the Jesus of Calvinism is a Jesus who came to save, not to merely make salvation possible. The cross revealed God's power to save, not His impotence. God was not frustrated at the cross. As Peter proclaimed after the Resurrection, "Him, being delivered by the determinate counsel and foreknowledge of God, ye have taken, and by wicked hands have crucified and slain" (Acts 2:23; KJV).

Along with the doctrines of grace, human responsibility to believe is another foundational doctrine, a hill on which to die. We must proclaim to every single person:

> All are sinners. All are dead in trespasses and sins. They are not sick and simply in need of help. Rather, they are dead and in need of life.

> Jesus Christ, God's Son, is a perfect, able and willing Savior of sinners, even the worst, yea, even the chief.

The Father and the Son have promised that all who know themselves to be sinners and who put their faith in Jesus Christ as Savior shall be received into favor, and none shall be cast out.

God has made faith and repentance a duty, requiring of every man who hears the gospel a serious and full casting of the soul upon Christ as an all-sufficient Savior. He is ready, willing and able to save all who come to God by Christ.

To the question, "What must I do to be saved?" we must respond to all who ask, "Believe on the Lord Jesus Christ and you will be saved." What does that mean? It means: (a) knowing that you are a sinner, (b) knowing that Christ has died for sinners, (c) abandoning all self-righteousness, self-confidence and self-effort as a means of salvation, (d) casting yourself wholly upon Christ for pardon and peace, (e) exchanging your natural enmity and rebellion against Christ for a spirit of grateful submission to the will of Christ through the renewing of your heart by the Holy Spirit.

It is these foundations that must be vigorously constructed in our churches. Upon the hearty preaching of these foundational doctrines, who knows but that God may be pleased to fan the flames of reformation fire.

Practical Suggestions for Local Church Reformation

The following practical suggestions for local church reformation are offered for your consideration. As I mentioned earlier, I learned these lessons the hard way.

Spiritual credibility. Don't try to reform a church until you have first earned spiritual credibility. This means you have to live what you teach in terms of holiness before you can even begin to teach it.

Accommodation. Study the biblical principle of accommodation. Accommodation is the willing restriction of the exercise of legitimate Christian liberty for the purpose of redeeming people whose consciences are bound by ignorance or misunderstanding resulting from man's fallen nature (cf. 1 Cor. 8:9-13). There is a fine line between accommodation and compromise. Compromise involves the relinquishment of Christian principles in order to accomplish one's purpose.

In contrast, accommodation involves the relinquishment of Christian liberty. This distinction must be carefully kept in mind, particularly with respect to the altar call and the general invitation system, which binds many Southern Baptists. You will need to find ways to engage in accommodation without compromise in your specific situation.[68]

Planning. Three questions should be asked, and carefully answered, before implementing change: What is the right, biblical thing to do? How should change be implemented? When should change be implemented? My advice is that you not try to do too much too soon. Many mistakes have been made by doing the right thing in the wrong way or at the wrong time. Especially do not get caught up in the trap of thinking controversy and conflict in and of themselves are the minister's badge of courage. Do not shy away from conflict when it comes (and it will come), but do everything you can from your end to avoid beginning it. Make sure it is the gospel that is offensive, not you.

Priorities. The principle of priorities must be applied. You can't change everything at once. Start with the major doctrines of the faith—God, Christ, and salvation. Don't get hung up on secondary matters such as eschatology. Find the essentials that must be changed in your situation, and focus on those.

The two churches. The principle of the two churches must be before you at all times. Keep in mind first the ideal church—the church, as it should be, conceived from the scriptures. Never abandon this. Consider also the real church—the church as it is— the one you look at 11:00 on Sunday morning. One must realize that the two shall never meet on earth, but you will find joy and satisfaction in narrowing the difference between them. When you look at the real church on Sunday morning, remember that your goal is to take small steps to move it toward the ideal one.

Church membership. Keep in mind the principle of church membership. Baptists have always believed in a regenerate church membership. Isaac Backus rightly said, "At all times the door of the church should be carefully kept [shut] against such as cannot give a satisfactory evidence of the work of God upon their souls, whereby they are united to Christ." At the same time, don't make church membership any narrower than the New Testament does. Don't make subscription to your favorite doctrinal tenets (even Calvinism) a requirement of membership.

Restraint. Remember the principle of restraint. Don't tackle the whole church at one time. Choose a few men who are sincere, teachable and spiritually minded and spend time with them in study and prayer. They will help you to reform. This principle is found in Titus 1: 5: "For this cause left I thee behind in Crete, that

88

thou shouldest set in order the things that are wanting and ordain elders in every city, as I had appointed thee" (KJV). Acts 14:23 likewise says, "And when they had ordained them elders in every church, and had prayed with fasting, they commended them to the Lord, on whom they believed" (KJV). See also Acts 11:30 ("Which also they did, and sent it to the elders by the hands of Barnabas and Saul; KJV); Acts 20:17,28 ("And from Miletus he sent to Ephesus, and called the elders of the church. Take heed therefore unto yourselves, and to all the flock, over which the Holy Ghost hath made you overseers, to feed the church of God, which he hath purchased with his own blood."; KJV).

Clarity. In the pulpit, don't use theological language that is not found in the Bible. Avoid terms such as Calvinism, reformed, doctrines of grace, particular redemption, etc. Most people will not know what you are talking about. Many that do will become inflamed against you. Teach your people the biblical truth of these doctrines without providing distracting labels for them.

Literature. Use sound literature, not indiscriminately, but wisely. Set up a book table in your church. Start with little things at first, that is, pamphlets and books with some doctrinal and experiential substance. Some possibilities are John Bunyan's *Pilgrim's Progress*, Martyn Lloyd-Jones's *Studies in the Sermon on the Mount*, Joseph Alleine's *A Sure Guide to Heaven*, Horatius Bonar's *Words to Winners of Souls*, and J. I. Packer's *Evangelism and the Sovereignty of God.*

When you use literature to foster reformation, keep in mind the three things you should know. First, you should know the books you give to others. Make sure you use books and literature that are consistent with the teachings of the Bible. Second, you should know the person to whom you give a book, including his needs and capacity. For example, when you are evangelizing, you may want to use Alleine's *Alarm to the Unconverted.* When you want to help a Christian understand the connection between the doctrines of grace and evangelism, you may want to use Packer's *Evangelism and the Sovereignty of God.* If a Christian is struggling with the role of the law in the life of a believer, use Samuel Bolton's *The True Bounds of Christian Freedom.* Do not give John Owen to someone who is not capable of using his works profitably. The point is, know the needs of the person to whom you give a book. Third, you should know the most serious areas of ignorance and the errors of our day. The doctor does not prescribe green pills to everyone; he gives medicine that is relevant to cure the problem. You must do the same. Finally, soak all the books you distribute in fervent prayer. You never know how a gift will assist someone come to faith or grow in their faith.

History. Check the history of your church to see if it has any early constitutions or declarations of faith. Often you will find, particularly in older churches, a statement expressing the doctrines which you desire to establish. A gracious appeal to such a document will help give you credibility. At least your congregation will know you are not coming from Mars. Stand behind these articles of faith. Stand behind our Baptist fathers, such as Bunyan, Spurgeon, Fuller, Boyce, Dagg, Broadus, Manly, W.B. Johnson, R.B.C. Howell and B.H. Carroll. The use of creeds and confessional statements is discussed in more detail in the next chapter.

Some additional points to remember are: Don't use the pulpit to scold people. You cannot scold people into reformation. Exercise common sense. Depend on the only weapons we have: prayer, preaching and teaching. Be sure that you understand the foundational doctrines of the faith and how they are related to each other and to your situation.

Above all, remember that the proper motives for reformation are love to God and concern for His glory, love for man and concern for his good; love for God's Holy Law as the only perfect, objective standard of righteousness; love for Christ and His Church; and love and compassion for sinners.

Counting the Cost

Men in every reformation were abused, misunderstood, misrepresented, reviled, persecuted, ostracized, and excommunicated from organized religion, suffered mental and physical agony, and often death. We too can expect no less today. We should not expect to see reformation without cost. Jesus said:

> And whosoever doth not bear his cross, and come after me, cannot be my disciple. For which of you, intending to build a tower, sitteth not down first, and counteth the cost, whether he have sufficient to finish it? Lest haply, after he hath laid the foundation, and is not able to finish it, all that behold it begin to mock him, saying, This man began to build and was not able to finish. (Luke 14:27-30; KJV).

What are the possible costs of reformation? We can think of a few.

Denominational popularity and public approval. The work of reformation is not the way to climb the denominational ladder.

Pain in tearing down rotting superstructures. The pastor involved in reformation will, at times, be called to that awful task of tearing down some false superstructure that had been built without a doctrinal foundation, that had been built by cheap, shallow, man-centered evangelism. This rotting edifice must be torn down before a solid foundation can be laid. In genuine reformation of a church, three things will always happen: some will leave, some will want to get rid of the preacher, and thank God, some will get right with God. There will be results—but not always saving results. Remember, in John 6 there were results—Jesus preached the crowd away.

Suffering at the hands of the unregenerate. The pastor involved in reformation may have to suffer at the hands of a large, unregenerate church membership, and especially from unregenerate and religiously ignorant deacons and leaders.

Suffering in the form of being misunderstood. The pastor involved in reformation may also have to suffer the pain of being misunderstood by even well-meaning, but misguided church leaders, fellow ministers, and more painful still, sometimes by their own loved ones (for example, wives who do not understand their husband's position).

Financial sacrifice. The pastor involved in reformation may have to sacrifice financially, especially in some cases where carnal and ignorant church leaders will use money as a threat to drive preachers from the pulpit.

But along with these and other costs there comes the joy of a conscience void of offence before God and man. Isn't that worth more than all the disapprobation that man can offer?

Since nothing in this mortal life is more important than true religion in the soul and in the church, reformation should be diligently sought after, and carefully looked into. It is not enough to pout and complain about what is wrong in the visible church, but we must be occupied in reforming and restoring what is right and biblical. Strengthen the things that remain.

CHAPTER FOUR

Teaching Others to Walk

The Use of Creeds and Confessions
In Local Church Reformation

Only be careful, and watch yourselves closely
so that you do not forget the things your eyes have seen
or let them slip from your heart as long as you live.
Teach them to your children and to their children after them.

Deut 4:9

The Future Generation

God is concerned about the future generations. Psalm 78:1-6 says:

> O my people, hear my teaching; listen to the words of my mouth. I will open my mouth in parables, I will utter hidden things, things from of old—what we have heard and known, what our fathers have told us. We will not hide them from their children; we will tell the next generation the praiseworthy deeds of the LORD, his power, and the wonders he has done. He decreed statutes for Jacob and established the law in Israel, which he commanded our forefathers to teach their children, so the next generation would know them, even the children yet to be born, and they in turn would tell their children. (NIV)

Psalm 145:4 similarly says: "One generation shall praise thy works to another, and shall declare thy mighty acts" (KJV).

One of the best teaching tools available in a reforming situation is the use of creeds, confessions and catechisms. Unfortunately, the use of these teaching tools has been lost in all-too many churches. Yet it is vitally important that we recover the use of our historical confessional statements. Reformation will not come if we do not know who we are and where we have come from. To this end, in my view, every reforming pastor should have on his shelf and in his church library a copy of Timothy and Denise George's collection of Baptist confessions of faith, covenants and catechisms.[69]

Definition Of Creeds, Confessions and Catechisms

It is often said that Baptists are not creedal people, that we have no creed but the Bible. This simply is not true. Baptists have often utilized confessions of faith, beginning with the General Baptists' Short Confession of Faith in Twenty Articles (1609) and the Particular Baptists' London Confession of 1644 and continuing to the Southern Baptist Convention's Baptist Faith and Message, recently amended in 2000.

We had better have some agreement as to the definitions of a "creed" and "confession." The word "creed" comes from the Latin word credo, and it simply means "I believe." Thus, when we say we believe certain things about Bible truth, we are saying we have a creed. A "confession of faith" is simply a declaration of those things believed by us. More specifically, it is a declaration of the manner in which a person, a number of people, or a church

95

understands the truth revealed in the Bible. A "catechism" is a statement of faith presented in the form of questions and answers, in a way that even children can understand.

It is important to have an inerrant Bible, but what good is an inerrant Bible if we do not know what it teaches or how to apply it to everyday practice? Many heretics and cults believe the Bible. However, it is their interpretation as to what the Bible teaches that has led them to their cultic and heretical views. Creeds and confessions come into existence to combat error. Invariably, they are born of controversy concerning what the Bible teaches in some respect.The Scriptures are from God, but the understanding of them belongs to the part of man.To the best of their ability, and with the aid of the Holy Spirit, men must interpret each particular part of Scripture separately, and then combine all that the Scriptures teach upon every subject into a consistent whole, and then adjust their teaching upon different subjects in mutual consistency as parts of a harmonious system. When you do this, you have a creed or confession of faith founded on Scripture alone.

Behind every creed and confession is Pilate's question, "What is truth?" What is the truth of God? The Confessions seek to answer that question assuming the truth is in the Bible and by appealing to the Bible as the only authoritative source of truth. When you ask a man the question, "What do you understand the Bible to teach?" and he answers you with a series of texts, he would be telling you nothing, unless at the same time he would state what he understands those texts to mean. When he proceeds to say what he believes these texts to mean he is giving you his creed and confession of faith. It may sound quite pious to say, "I have no creed but Christ, and no textbook but the Bible," but which Christ are you talking about? There are a thousand Christs on the religious market, but they are not all the Christ of the Bible. It is likewise with the statement "The Bible is my textbook." Most religious crackpots or cultists would make the same claim. Therefore, someone must articulate what the "textbook" teaches or means, and how it applies to faith and practice. This is why the great creeds came on the historic scene. The Westminster Confession of Faith and the First and Second London Baptist Confessions of Faith refute the heresies of Arianism, Socinianism, Gnosticism, Pelagianism, Semi-Pelagianism, Universalism, Arminianism and Antinomianism without even mentioning them by name.

A creed or confession of faith is not the voice of divine truth, but the echo of that voice from men who have heard the utterance of divine truth, men who have felt the power of divine truth, and who have answered the call of divine truth.

96

Do Baptists Have Creeds Or Confessions?

It is evident that every Baptist must have a creed because every Baptist has a statement of belief. Nevertheless, let me answer this question more specifically from Cathcart's Baptist Encyclopedia, p. 293:

> "Every thinking man has a Creed about politics, religion, and the best manner of conducting the business with which he is most familiar. It may not be printed, it may not be communicated in words except in special cases, but it surely exists in all intelligent minds. And if the reader can remember a denomination without an avowed Confession of Faith, he will find that in that community there is an understood creed just as real, and as well known by those familiar with its people and its teachings, as if everyone of its members carried a printed copy of it in his hand. Baptists have always gloried in the fact that the Bible was their creed, and at the same time, for centuries they have had published Confessions of Faith."

Many Baptists are not aware that historically, Baptists have always had creeds and confessions, and presently, all do have a creed and confession of faith. One of the best known (and one of the most biblical) Baptist confessions of faith is the London Confession of 1689, which was an improvement and enlargement of two previous Baptist Confessions of 1644 and 1646. This confession of faith was in turn slightly modified by early American Baptists to become the Philadelphia Confession of Faith. The Philadelphia Association adopted it in 1744. Southern Baptists have their roots in this association. The mother of both of these confessions is the best known of all confessions, the Westminster Confession. The major differences between the Westminster Confession and the Baptist Confession of 1689 are on the subjects of baptism, the Lord's Supper and church government.

While the Baptist Confession of 1689 is the preferable teaching tool, for congregations in the beginning stages of reform, you can even use the 2000 Baptist Faith and Message to teach doctrine to your congregation. Get your people to think about statements like the following:

> Only the grace of God can bring man into His holy fellowship and enable man to fulfill the creative purpose of God (Article III, Man).

> Regeneration, or the new birth, is a work of God's grace whereby believers become new creatures in Christ Jesus. It

is a change of heart wrought by the Holy Spirit through conviction of sin, to which the sinner responds in repentance
toward God and faith in the Lord Jesus Christ. Repentance
and faith are inseparable experiences of grace (Article IV,
Salvation).

Election is the gracious purpose of God, according to which
He regenerates, justifies, sanctifies, and glorifies sinners. It
is consistent with the free agency of man, and comprehends
all the means in connection with the end (Article V, God's
Purpose of Grace).[62]

Using these statements, ask your people things like:

What does it mean to say that only God's grace brings man into
fellowship with him?
Whose work is regeneration—God's or man's?
What is the place of repentance in salvation, and what position
does the confessional statement take on the so-called "Lordship
salvation" controversy?
Which comes first, election or justification?

By using a trusted document like the 2000 Baptist Faith and
Message to frame issues in this fashion and to get your people
thinking theologically, you can then take them to Scripture to
teach them what the Bible says about the doctrines of grace. Once
a core group is convinced, you can introduce them to the fuller
treatment of these doctrines in the older confessions.

C. H. Spurgeon On Confessions

In 1855, the "prince of preachers" had been the minister of the
New Park Street Chapel, London, only a few months when he
determined to strengthen the doctrinal foundations of his own and
other churches by reissuing the 1689 Baptist Confession.

In doing so, Spurgeon gave some practical words of advice to
his church as to the right use of confessions. His words continue
to be relevant for us. "This little volume" he wrote, "is not issued
as an authoritative rule, or code of faith, whereby you are to be fet-
tered, but as an assistance to you in controversy, a confirmation
in faith, and a means of edification in righteousness. Here the
younger members of our church will have a body of divinity in
small compass, and by means of the Scriptural proofs, will be
ready to give a reason for the hope that is in them. Be not
ashamed of your faith; remember it is the ancient gospel of martyrs, confessors, reformers, and saints. It is the truth of

God, against which the gates of hell cannot prevail. Let your lives adorn your faith; let your example adorn your Creed. Above all, live in Christ Jesus, and walk in Him, giving credence to no teaching but that which is manifestly approved of Him, and owned by the Holy Spirit. Cleave fast to the Word of God which is here mapped out for you."

Creeds, Confessions And The Bible

To those who say, "Creeds and confessions are just the works of men," we find ourselves in hearty agreement with their statement. This does not nullify the point, however. If men will not be aided by the doctrine elaborated and defined by the respected creeds and confessions, they must make up their own creed by their own unaided wisdom.

Charles Hodge says:

> The real question is not, as often pretended, between the Word of God and the creed of man, but between the tried and proved faith of the collective body of God's people, and the private judgment and the unassisted wisdom of the repudiator of creeds.
>
> As we would have anticipated, it is a matter of fact that the Church has advanced very gradually in this work of the accurate interpretation of Scripture and definition of the great doctrines, which compose the system of truth it reveals. The attention of the Church has been specially directed to the study of one doctrine in one age, and of another doctrine in another age. And as she has thus gradually advanced in the clear discrimination of gospel truth, she has at different periods set down an accurate statement of the results of her new attainments in a Creed or Confession of Faith, for the purpose of preservation and popular instruction. In the meantime, heretics spring up on all occasions, who pervert the Scriptures, who exaggerate certain aspects of the truth and deny others equally essential, and thus in effect turn the truth of God into a lie. The Church is forced, therefore, on the great principle of self-preservation, to form such accurate definitions of every particular doctrine misrepresented as shall include the whole truth and exclude all error; and to make such comprehensive exhibitions of the system of revealed

99

truth as a whole that no one part shall be either unduly diminished or exaggerated, but the true proportion of the whole be preserved. At the same time, provision must be made for ecclesiastical discipline, and to secure the real cooperation of those who profess to work together in the same cause; so that public teachers in the same communion may not contradict one another, and the one pull down what the other is striving to build up. Formularies must also be prepared, representing as far as possible the common consent, and clothed with public authority, for the instruction of the members of the Church, and especially of the children.

Creeds and confessions, therefore, have been found necessary in all ages and branches of the Church, and, when not abused, have been useful for the following purposes: (1) To mark, disseminate, and preserve the attainments made in the knowledge of Christian truth by any branch of the Church in any crisis of its development. (2) To discriminate the truth from the glosses of false teachers, and to present it in its integrity and true proportions. (3) To act as the basis of ecclesiastical fellowship among those so nearly agreed as to be able to labor together in harmony. (4) To be used as instruments in the great work of popular instruction.

The Value And Necessity Of A Confession

Confessions and creeds form a bond and union among those who hold the same views. Cannot every true Baptist and every true Christian say:

> I believe in God the Father Almighty, Maker of heaven and earth.
> I believe in Jesus Christ his only Son our Lord.
> I believe Jesus Christ was conceived by the Holy Ghost
> and was born of the virgin Mary.
> I believe that Jesus Christ suffered under Pontius Pilate.
> I believe Jesus Christ was crucified on the cross.
> I believe Jesus Christ was dead and buried.
> I believe Jesus Christ rose again from the dead.
> I believe Jesus Christ ascended into heaven,
> and sits on the right hand of God the Father Almighty.
> I believe Jesus Christ shall come again to judge the quick and the dead.

Is there a true Baptist that is not willing to say, "I believe these truths because they are clearly taught in the Bible?" Well, if you can say, "I believe these statements," then you are a creedal person, unless words and definitions mean nothing to you.

By this creed, Unitarians, Liberals, Jehovah's Witnesses, and all cults exclude themselves from such a bond. The late Walter Martin, a Southern Baptist, who taught at Simon Greenleaf School of Law and was an authority on cults, defined a cult as, "A religion centered around a man who has his own interpretation of the Bible." It should not, therefore, seem strange that usually it is latitudinarians and heretics that object to the historic creeds and confessions.

Creeds are neither inspired nor authoritative. They are not, in and of themselves, an absolute certainty of truth. Instead, they depict with absolute certainty what certain individuals believe the Scriptures teach. This does not infringe upon liberty of conscience. One of the reasons for the religious confusion and divisions in Christendom today is there is no creed to bind Christians together.

Thus, creeds are necessary to clearly set out what the Bible teaches on a given subject. Confessions, similarly, are useful in propagating and preserving biblical knowledge gained by our fathers. The essence of Christian duty is to be a witness and a propagator of God's truth. This requires a public definition of the exact identity of that to which the Christian is a witness. When we give testimony we express our creed in words. Peter's creed was, "I believe that thou art the Christ, the Son of the living God."

The Bible is full of short or mini-creeds. Romans 10:9, 1 Corinthians 12:3 and Philippians 2:11 all confess Jesus is Lord. Creeds are absolutely necessary to define our beliefs.

All the heresies that the Westminster and London Confessions refute reappear in the history of the Church under different names and dress. Because of the same depraved nature in man, and the sameness of the human mind, there is a perpetual recurring tendency to reproduce old error. Hence, creeds are necessary to expose false teaching and teachers. Confessions furnish a fixed standard by which to test or judge them.

Creeds furnish an objective standard to teach, promote, and preserve God's truth in the earth. As witnesses of God's truth we must state to the world what that truth is. Confessions and creeds are a method of bringing the whole Bible to bear on specific subjects.

Dangers Of Creeds And Confessions.

We would be remiss if we did not mention some of the dangers of creeds and confessions.

One of the chief dangers of creeds and confessions is using them to bind the conscience. One reason why some Baptists have traditionally shied away from the term "creed," is that denominational creeds were historically used by others to force their particular beliefs upon Baptists. Creeds must never be used to bind the conscience. Creeds can only bind the conscience so far as they are biblical, and, they bind only those who voluntarily subscribe to them.

Another danger is allowing creeds to usurp the place of authority that belongs to the Bible. We do not worship the creeds. The Bible alone is our final authority and standard. By it we must prove all things. We must not exalt our creeds above the Bible or treat them as equal to the Bible. Creeds are the products of men. However, the respected creeds are the products of many holy, competent, and seasoned men. These creeds have proved a safeguard for Christians.

They are not independent assertions of truth. They are derived from, and subordinate to, the Bible as the only source and standard of Christian authority.

In fact, the creeds and confessions themselves warn against the dangers of creeds. The Philadelphia Confession of Faith declares in Chapter 21, part 2:

> God alone is Lord of the conscience, and hath left it free from the doctrines and commandments of men which are in any thing contrary to his word or not contained in it. So that to believe such doctrines, or obey such commands out of conscience is to betray true liberty of conscience; and the requiring of an implicit faith, and absolute and blind obedience, is to destroy liberty of conscience and season also."[71]

Beware Of Those Who Knock The Tried And Proven Creeds

Beware of those who knock the historic creeds. Who are they?

Those who know nothing of their history, purpose, value, or their biblical substance.

Heretics. All heretics speak against the creeds. (Notice we did not say everyone who speaks against the creeds is a heretic.)

Liberals who do not believe the Bible. They have no use for creeds that define objectively the doctrines of the Bible.

Those who want to promote their own creed.

Baptists have always gloried that the Bible was their creed and at the same time, for centuries, they have published confessions of faith.

[1] R. M. Dudley, "The Distinctive Baptist Way" in *Baptist Why and Why Not* (Broadman, 1900, reprinted Nashville, TN: Broadman & Holman, 1996), 26-27.

[2] L. Russ Bush and Tom J. Nettles, *Baptists and the Bible* (Chicago, IL: Moody Press, 1980), 51. Bush and Nettles note that the phrase "contained in the Canonicall Scriptures" does not refer to a belief that God's words are intermixed with other words, but could as well be stated "limited to the Canonicall Scriptures." *Ibid*, 53. Indeed, when the confession was republished in 1651, it was accompanied by an essay against Quakers which declared that the Bible contains "the whole Minde, will, and Law of God, for us and all Saints to believe and practise throughout all ages." *Ibid*, 56.

[3] *Ibid*, 62-63. Significantly, the expression that the Bible is "the only sufficient" rule of knowledge, faith and obedience is an addition from the Westminster Confession of Faith, from which the Second London Confession is modeled. *Ibid*, 65.

[4] *Ibid*, 64.

[5] *Ibid*, 105.

[6] *Ibid*, 107.

[7] *Ibid*, 78.

[8] *Ibid*, 225.

[9] *Ibid*, 387.

[10] See Benjamin B. Warfield, "Calvinism" in *The Works of Benjamin B. Warfield*, vol. 5 (Grand Rapids, MI: Baker Book House, reprinted 2000), 354-355.

[11] John L. Dagg, *Manual of Theology* (1857, reprinted, Harrisonburg, VA: Gano Books, 1990).

[12] James P. Boyce, *Abstract of Systematic Theology* (1887, reprinted Hanford, CA: den Dulk Christian Foundation, n.d.), 367-68.

[13] *Ibid*, 348.

[14] *Ibid*, 340.

[15] Dagg, *Manual of Theology*, 287.

[16] We have borrowed these words from Bishop Ryle's *Old Paths*

(Carlisle, PA: Banner of Truth Trust, 1999 reprint), vi-vii.

[17] See Iain Murray, *D. Martyn Lloyd-Jones – The Fight of Faith 1939-1981* (Edinburgh, Scotland: The Banner of Truth Trust, 1990), 72-75.

[18] For a sampling of excellent books discussing the current evangelical crisis, see David F. Wells, *No Place for Truth, Or Whatever Happened to Evangelical Theology* (Grand Rapids, MI: Eerdmans, 1993); *God in the Wasteland* (Grand Rapids, MI: Eerdmans, 1994); *Losing Our Virtue* (Grand Rapids, MI: Eerdmans, 1998); John H. Armstrong, ed. *The Coming Evangelical Crisis: Current Challenges to the Authority of Scripture and the Gospel* (Chicago, IL: Moody Press, 1996).

[19] Quoted from Iain H. Murray, "Billy Graham: Catalyst for Change" *The Banner of Truth*, Issue 438, 9.

[20] Quoted in John Dart, "Protestant Churches Join the Fold, Fill Pews with Saturday Services," *Los Angeles Times* (15 September 1991), B3.

[21] John MacArthur, *Ashamed of the Gospel* (Wheaton, IL: Crossway Books, 1993), 47.

[22] Marv Knox, "Patterson Keynotes Conference on Rearticulating Fundamentals" *Baptist Standard* (March 8, 2000).

[23] For an extended discussion of this topic, see "Appendix A – A Perspective on the Spiritual Drift in Hymnody" in Michael Horton, *In the Face of God* (Dallas, TX: Word Publishing, 1996), 195-201; see also Michael Foust, "Shallow Choruses Have Replaced Scriptural Hymns, Panelists Say" *Baptist Press* (April 18, 2000).

[24] Quoted from "News" in *Founders Journal* (Summer 1990), issue 2 [republished Founders Online CD-ROM].

[25] See Joel R. Beeke, *Puritan Evangelism - A Biblical Approach* (Grand Rapids, MI: Reformation Heritage Books, 1999), 24-29. See also Walter J. Chantry, *Today's Gospel: Authentic or Synthetic* (Edinburgh: Banner of Truth Trust, 1970).

[26] Wells, *No Place For Truth*, 96.

[27] Thomas J. Nettles, *By His Grace and For His Glory* (Grand Rapids, MI: Baker, 1986), 31-35.

[28] Mark Noll, *A History of Christianity in the United States and Canada* (Grand Rapids, MI: Eerdmans, 1992), 365.

29 *Ibid*, 368-69.

30 A.T. Robertson, *Life and Letters of John A. Broadus* (Harrisonburg, VA: Gano Books, 1987), 396-97.

31 This assumption was tested in the 1870s when Southern Seminary professor C. H. Toy abandoned the orthodox view of biblical inspiration and began to teach higher critical theories. Toy resigned under pressure in 1879. See Timothy George, "Introduction" to Basil Manly, Jr., *The Bible Doctrine of Inspiration* (Nashville, TN: Broadman & Holman, 1995), 6-9.

32 E.C. Dargan, *The Doctrines of Our Faith* (Nashville, TN: Sunday School Board, Southern Baptist Convention, 1905), 143.

33 J.M. Frost, "Introduction" *Baptist Why and Why Not* (Broadman, 1900, reprinted Nashville, TN: Broadman & Holman, 1996), 15.

34 William A. Mueller, *A History of Southern Baptist Theological Seminary* (Nashville, TN: Broadman Press, 1959), 177.

35 Quoted in Timothy George, "Introduction," *Baptist Why and Why Not* (Broadman & Holman, 1996), 2.

36 Noll, *A History of Christianity in the United States and Canada*, 372.

37 R. Albert Mohler, "Introduction" to *The Axioms of Religion* (reprinted Broadman & Holman, 1997), 7-8.

38 *Ibid*, 9.

39 Sean Michael Lucas, "Christianity at the Crossroads: E. Y. Mullins, J. Gresham Machen, and the Challenge of Modernism" *The Southern Baptist Journal of Theology*, vol. 3, no. 3 (Winter 1999) (article available on the internet from the Southern Baptist Theological Seminary website).

40 David S. Dockery, *Christian Scripture* (Broadman & Holman, 1995), 194.

41 See Mohler, "Introduction," 10.

42 Mohler, "Introduction," 11; Dockery, *Christian Scripture*, 201. Cf. E. Y. Mullins, *Why Is Christianity True?* (Philadelphia, PA: American Baptist Publication Society, 1905), 69-71.

43 Quoted in James C. Hefley, *The Conservative Resurgence in the Southern Baptist Convention* (Hannibal Books, 1992), 20.

44 Herschel H. Hobbs & E. Y. Mullins, *The Axioms of Religion* (Nashville, TN: Broadman Press, 1978), 71-72.

45 Mohler, "Introduction" to *The Axioms of Religion*, 25-26.

46 This section is penned by Matthew Allen; therefore, co-author Ernest Reisinger is referred to in the third person.

47 C. H. Spurgeon, *Autobiography – The Full Harvest*, vol. 2 (Edinburgh: The Banner of Truth Trust, 1973), 45.

48 Quoted in "Publisher's Introduction" to Boyce, *Abstract*, xiv.

49 *Ibid*, xiv, xx.

50 Quoted in Nettles, *By His Grace and For His Glory*, 196.

51 "Publisher's Introduction, *Abstract of Systematic Theology*, pp. viii-ix, xv-xix, xx.

52 *Ibid*, xxi-xxii.

53 Quoted from a transcript of a taped lecture delivered at Southwestern Baptist Theological Seminary, reprinted in Ernest C. Reisinger, *Reforming a Local Church* (Pensacola, FL: Chapel Library, n.d.), 2-3.

54 Quoted from dust cover, John L. Dagg, *Manual of Theology* (Harrisonburg, VA: 1990).

55 Tom Ascol, "Raison d'etre: An Editorial Introduction," *Founders Journal* (Spring 1990) [republished Founders Online CD-ROM].

56 Tom Ascol, "Where Do We Go From Here," *Founders Journal* (Summer, 1990), Issue 2 [republished Founders Online CD-ROM].

57 William R. Estep, "Doctrines Lead to Dunghill, Prof Warns," *Texas Baptist Standard*, 26 March 1997, reprinted in *Founders Journal* (Summer, 1997).

58 Tom Ascol, "Do Doctrines Really Lead to Dunghill," *Founders Journal* (Summer, 1997).

59 R. Albert Mohler, "The Reformation of Doctrine and the Renewal of the Church" *Founders Journal* (Summer, 1997).

60 Roger Nicole, "An Open Letter to Dr. William Estep," *Founders Journal* (Summer, 1997).

61 All quotations from Art Toalston, "Editor's Critique of Calvinism Prompts Challenges in Return," *Baptist Press* (September 19, 1997).

62 All quotations from "Patterson: Calvinism OK but Wrong," *Baptist Standard* (November 24, 1999).

63 Edward E. Plowman, "Choosing Calvinism?" *World Magazine* (June 19, 1999); Letter to "Mailbag" *World Magazine* (July 24, 1999).

64 Letter from Adrian Rogers to Ernest Reisinger dated February 18, 2000,

copy on file with authors.

[65] Mark Wingfield, "Gage: Baptist churches not reaching 'pagan' culture" *Baptist Standard* (April 24, 2000).

[66] This chapter is penned principally by Ernest Reisinger.

[67] John Calvin, *Institutes of the Christian Religion*, Ford Lewis Battles, translator (Philadelphia, PA: Westminster Press, 1960), 593, 597 (3.3.1, 3.3.5).

[68] There is a little pamphlet on this subject (*The Principle of Biblical Accommodation as Applied to the Invitation System*), and an excellent message on cassette by Thomas K. Ascol available through The Christian Gospel Foundation, 521 Wildwood Parkway, Cape Coral, FL 33904, or Dr. Thomas K. Ascol, Grace Baptist Church, 204 SW 11th Place, Cape Coral, FL 33991. The message on biblical accommodation is also available on the Founder Online CD. For more information, contact Founders Press, P.O. Box 150931, Cape Coral, Florida 33915.

[69] Timothy George, *Baptist Confessions, Covenants, and Catechisms* (Nashville, TN: Broadman & Holman, 1996).

[70] At the 2000 Southern Baptist Convention in Orlando, Florida, the delegates approved certain modifications to the Baptist Faith and Message. One of those revisions was the addition of the word "justifies" to Article V. This is an extremely positive development. Based on this modification, the Southern Baptist Convention has rejected in its confessional statement the unbiblical idea that God's election is based on foreseen faith. Instead, the Convention has adopted the biblical view that justification, as well as regeneration, sanctification and glorification, is "according to" God's election.

[71] The Philadelphia Confession of Faith (1742), quoted in George, *Baptist Confessions, Covenants and Catechisms*, 57.